Nonprofit Management & Leadership

VOLUME 17   NUMBER 2   WINTER 2006

CASE
MANDEL CENTER FOR
NONPROFIT ORGANIZATIONS

*We gratefully acknowledge the generous support and
encouragement of the Mandel Foundation.*

NONPROFIT MANAGEMENT AND LEADERSHIP (Print ISSN: 1048-6682; Online ISSN: 1542-7854) is a quarterly journal published by Wiley Subscription Services, Inc., A Wiley Imprint, at Jossey-Bass, 989 Market Street, San Francisco, California 94103-1741.

PERIODICALS Postage Paid at San Francisco, California, and at additional mailing offices. POSTMASTER: Send address changes to Nonprofit Management and Leadership, Jossey-Bass, 989 Market Street, San Francisco, CA 94103-1741.

NONPROFIT MANAGEMENT AND LEADERSHIP is indexed in ABI/Inform Database (ProQuest), Business Periodicals Index/Abstracts (HW Wilson), Cambridge Scientific Abstracts (CSA/CIG), CIJE: Current Index to Journals in Education (ERIC), Current Abstracts (EBSCO), Educational Administration Abstracts (Sage), Human Resource Abstracts (Sage), IBSS: International Bibliography of the Social Sciences (LSE), Journal of Economic Literature/EconLit (AEA), Philanthropic Studies Index, Psychological Abstracts/PsycINFO (APA), Public Administration Abstracts (Sage), Social Services Abstracts (CSA/CIG), SocINDEX (EBSCO), and Sociological Abstracts (CSA/CIG)

SUBSCRIPTION rates: For institutions, agencies, and libraries: $212 per year in the United States, $252 per year in Canada and Mexico, and $286 per year in the rest of the world; for individuals: $80 per year in the United States, Canada, and Mexico, and $104 per year in the rest of the world. Prices subject to change.

Cover and publication design by Victor Ichioka.

www.josseybass.com

Nonprofit Management & Leadership

Volume 17   Number 2   Winter 2006

DEPARTMENTS

CALL FOR PAPERS

Nonprofit Management and Leadership
A Journal on Management, Governance, Leadership, and Policy
of Nonprofit Organizations for Practitioners and Scholars

Contributions are sought from interested researchers and practitioners. Submitted papers should be based on original research or on theory of organizations and management and should be written in a jargon-free, nontechnical style accessible to managers, trustees, and other leaders of nonprofit and voluntary organizations and to academic researchers and teachers from a variety of disciplines and professions. Papers should focus on some aspect of nonprofit organization management, governance, leadership, or policy, and may include reports on research, literature reviews, case studies, and theoretical and analytical essays. Papers on governance, management of human resources, resource development and financial management, strategy and management of change, and organizational effectiveness are especially encouraged. Papers should be 4,000 to 5,000 words long and double-spaced. A detailed style guide is available on request.

Papers for the journal's occasional "From the Field" section can be based primarily on experience rather than on formal research design, and often are written by practitioners. Case studies of strategic or other interest to nonprofit researchers and practitioners can also be submitted for consideration; they may be either research or teaching cases and should be five to ten pages long and double-spaced. They should pose ethical and strategic management dilemmas of concern to nonprofit managers and leaders. Letters critiquing or commenting on previously published articles are also welcome.

All papers submitted to *Nonprofit Management and Leadership* are subject to rigorous peer review. Researchers and practitioners willing to review manuscripts should send a letter of interest and a current copy of their curriculum vitae to the editor at the address provided below.

Nonprofit Management and Leadership seeks to reflect the international growth and diversity of management, leadership, and third-sector issues in Europe, Asia, Latin America, and Africa. Manuscripts on topics of interest to an international audience of NGO management and leadership researchers and practitioners are invited from authors residing outside North America. An extensive panel of non-U.S. reviewers and associate editors is available. Submissions originating outside the United States are reviewed by experts familiar with the topic and country of origin.

To discuss paper topics with the editor via e-mail, contact Roger A. Lohmann at rlohmann@wvu.edu. Electronic submissions in MS Word format are preferred; e-mail manuscript queries and file attachments to Kathleen Mills, managing editor, at NMLjournal@case.edu. Otherwise, send one copy of the manuscript (with accompanying electronic copy on disk, if possible) via the post to Roger A. Lohmann, Mandel Center for Nonprofit Organizations, Case Western Reserve University, 10900 Euclid Avenue, Cleveland, OH 44106-7167.

EDITOR'S NOTES

THIS ISSUE is a thematic one, devoted entirely to consideration of a single theme: values, passions, and ethics in the nonprofit sector. The guest editors, Joyce Rothschild and Carl Milofsky, are recognized scholars with extensive published work on nonprofit and third-sector topics. As they note in their introduction, "The Centrality of Values, Passions, and Ethics in the Nonprofit Sector," this special issue of *Nonprofit Management and Leadership* arose from discussions within the Association for Research on Nonprofit Organizations and Voluntary Action section on community and grassroots associations. It represents an effort to reach beyond some of the usual management preoccupations and broaden the range of nonprofit management and leadership conversations.

As always, feedback from readers is welcome.

Roger A. Lohmann
Editor

WILEY
InterScience®
DISCOVER SOMETHING GREAT

ANNOUNCING THE 2006 RECIPIENT OF

THE EDITORS' PRIZE
for

The Best Scholarly Paper in
Nonprofit Management and Leadership
Volume 15

The Mandel Center for Nonprofit Organizations, the editorial and advisory boards of *Nonprofit Management and Leadership*, and Jossey-Bass are pleased to announce that the Editors' Prize for Volume 15 has been awarded to

William A. Brown
for his article
"Exploring the Association Between Board and Organizational Performance in Nonprofit Organizations"

Professor Brown's study investigated six dimensions of effective board performance in relation to three theoretical explanations (agency theory, resource dependency theory, and group/decision process theory) of how board governance activities potentially influence organizational performance. Survey research findings revealed that strategic contributions from the board are more robust in organizations with higher financial performance. Organizations judged to be higher performing also reported having high-performing boards across all dimensions. In particular, the interpersonal dimension provided a unique explanation of judgments of organizational performance. This dimension is "an area of less prominence in the practitioner literature than, say, the monitoring function," writes Brown, "but this study suggests that time spent building an effective board as a team is not wasted."

William A. Brown, associate professor in the Bush School of Government and Public Service at Texas A&M University, teaches graduate courses on nonprofit organizations and program evaluation. He holds an M.A. and Ph.D. in organizational psychology from Claremont Graduate University and a B.S. in education from Northeastern University. Dr. Brown has worked with numerous organizations in the direct provision of services, consulting, and board governance. His research focuses on nonprofit governance and organizational effectiveness.

The Editors' Prize is awarded annually for the best article published in NML during the preceding subscription year. Winners receive a $1,000 cash prize courtesy of the Mandel Center for Nonprofit Organizations and $1,000 in books from Jossey-Bass.

Winners are selected by the members of the editorial and advisory boards of NML. Criteria are based on the author's contribution to knowledge in the field of nonprofit management, the quality of the writing and analysis, and the usefulness of the information for the practice of nonprofit management and leadership.

The Centrality of Values, Passions, and Ethics in the Nonprofit Sector

Joyce Rothschild, Carl Milofsky

NONPROFIT ORGANIZATIONS are grounded in their members' values and passions and sustained by the bonds of trust that develop within and between them. They are the organizational expression of their members' ethical stance toward the world: nonprofit organizations, by way of their very existence and practices, convey a public statement of what their members see as a better, more caring, or more just world. This is why they come into being in the first place. Business firms, by way of contrast, are fueled by a profit motive. If market opportunities take them away from their original products or services and toward some new product line, this is accepted and even considered a sign of good management so long as returns on equity improve and profit accumulation grows. Public agencies are guided by statutory dictate: laws that are passed and signed by representatives of the electorate. Nonprofit organizations have neither of these limitations or anchors. They are born of human needs perceived but not served by existing markets or government statute. To understand the nonprofit sector, we must understand the substantive values and ethics that people hold—that is, the qualities of life they want to realize that are not being achieved through profit-seeking or governmental organizations.

Once we remind ourselves of the substantive values that give rise to nonprofit efforts, we can begin to grasp the more involving, discursive, and democratic form of organization that the nonprofit sector invites. Indeed, part of what people may want to accomplish in nonprofit organizations may have as much to do with constructing an authentically democratic form of organization in which ordinary people get to practice democracy and voice as it does with the desire to achieve specific goals (Rothschild and Whitt, 1986). As such, the processes of the organization may prove to be as important to the participants as the goals, and this may be an equally important way in which nonprofit organizations distinguish themselves from for-profit or state agencies.

In a world of resource scarcity, however, and as they age, nonprofit organizations have been noted to become more bureaucratic and to adopt practices and goals indistinguishable from those in their environment (Wood, 1992). They may come to sell products and services in a market, just as for-profit enterprises do. They have been known to accept grants that are attractive and available but do not fit their mission. They are subject to the pressures of organizational isomorphism (DiMaggio and Powell, 1988) and follow the fashions of their institutional fields rather than the logical dictates of their mission and core values. They are often scrutinized by the public and regulated by government or institutional associations, and as a result, they may adapt to fit conventionally accepted images of proper management style and organizational form. In all of these ways, hierarchical and bureaucratic forms of organization from the government and for-profit sectors may end up being imported to the nonprofit sector, all in the name of "maturity," "appropriateness," "growth," and even "accountability."

> *To understand the nonprofit sector, we must understand the substantive values and ethics that people hold.*

This special issue of *Nonprofit Management and Leadership* asks under what conditions nonprofit organizations can manage to stick to, and deepen, the specific values, passions, and ethics from which they sprang, not how they can "mature" into full-blown bureaucratic organizations with extensive rules, procedures, and professional staffs. We ask how the egalitarian ethos and the commitment of volunteers who animate the beginnings of so many of these organizations can be sustained. In our view, this question ought to be among the central issues of scholarship related to nonprofit management and theory, and through this special issue of *NML* we hope to stimulate further research and dialogue on it. This special issue grew out of an effort by members of the Community and Grassroots Organizations Section of the Association for Research on Nonprofit Organizations and Voluntary Action to present research that helps to frame and understand this area of discussion.

Research on for-profit businesses does not fail to study the relative success of such organizations in terms of market position, return on equity, profit margins, or growth of earnings. Recent discussions of business organizations may add to the analysis newer metrics having to do with corporate social responsibility, but most business analysts would consider the latter irrelevant if it diminished profit growth. Government agencies are held accountable to their purposes, as set forth in statutes, and employees are expected to administer or implement the law whether or not they personally believe in it. This presents a formidable impediment to employee voice, much less worker empowerment and self-management, in the public sector (Behn, 2005). Indeed, business enterprises that depend on their employees for creative ideas and inventions have been much quicker to grasp the motivational advantages of a less hierarchical and more democratic workplace and thus engaged workforce, and they have gone much further down this road than has the public sector (Rothschild, 2000). The nonprofit sector, however, stands alone in appealing only to those who believe in the qualitative purposes of the organization. Why else volunteer or seek employment with a nonprofit organization? The other sectors of society generally pay more and rely not at all on volunteers to get their work tasks done. It would be most unusual if employers in the for-profit or public sectors even asked individuals during the hiring process whether they believed in the profit motive or in the statute that defined the public agency. Only in the nonprofit organization is commitment to a substantive value a determinant of employment or volunteer service (Oster, 1995).

Despite the substantive values that form the premise of the nonprofit sector and motivate the beginnings of these organizations, the values and ethics of participants are understudied and often overlooked in the research on nonprofit organizations. This may be partly due to the relative methodological difficulty of getting a handle on values, passions, and ethics. Surely the metrics of performance used in the for-profit world and even in the public sector are easier to measure. This, however, is not the whole story, because as a field we could do a better job of assessing the extent to which nonprofit organizations accomplish their original missions. Students of for-profit enterprise do not generally forget to look at profits and losses, just as students of public sector organizations do not forget the statute-based purposes of those organizations, but we believe that too often practitioners and students of nonprofits get sidetracked by a lens borrowed from the for-profit (dominant) sector. In this way, nonprofit practitioners may come to think that they need to emulate the formal and hierarchical organizational structures that, as Weber warned over a hundred years ago, can only eliminate substantive values from the effective equation. Concerns with efficiency can come to crowd out devotion to substantive purpose, bringing in place of those qualitative purposes "accountability" data that can be used to justify and protect the organization but add little to its actual services and formal rules and procedures that only discourage formerly devoted volunteers and staff from participating.

> *The nonprofit sector stands alone in appealing only to those who believe in the qualitative purposes of the organization.*

We frequently hear lip-service paid to the importance of the qualitative mission or purpose in a nonprofit organization. However, because many nonprofit scholars are most interested in what David Horton Smith (1997a, 1997b) calls "large, paid-staff nonprofits," the realistic target of work in the field often has shifted to how nonprofit organizations can generate enough resources to survive and how they can adopt top-down managerial styles that make drift from the founding mission (Sills, 1957; Jeavons, 1994) the norm rather than the exception. Within this context, we ask in this special volume of *NML* what it means to wed values and structure.

We begin this special issue with a fascinating account of Alcoholics Anonymous (AA) written by Thomasina Borkman.

Borkman shows how the founding conception, specific history, and leadership of AA combined to develop an organization where empathic and egalitarian values are not just spoken, but are key to the very method by which the organization helps people. As she shows, the shared experience of equals is the essence of the method and purpose of AA, without which it would be unable to stir personal transformation. As AA wedded its original values and purposes to its organizational structure, it ended up establishing a decentralized, experience-based, egalitarian method and template emulated by hundreds of other self-help organizations.

In the next article in this issue, Elizabeth Hoffmann analyzes worker cooperatives, pointing out that they are hybrid organizations. Like nonprofit organizations, they are set up to serve social needs and substantive values. Like businesses, they seek to produce a livelihood for their worker-owner members, but unlike conventional businesses, they are not profit maximizing. They have social purposes and egalitarian values as well. Hoffmann shows in her analysis of workers in cooperative enterprises in comparison to workers in conventional capitalist-owned enterprises that the cooperative organizations engender considerably more loyalty. This may be "ironic," as she puts it, because while greater loyalty leads people to work harder for the co-op than they would for a conventional firm that they did not own, it may also lead them to express more grievance about or criticism of the co-op. Hoffmann's work reminds us that the greater commitment and loyalty that can be generated in nonprofit organizations should not be expected to produce more quietude or conformity.

> *The greater commitment and loyalty that can be generated in nonprofit organizations should not be expected to produce more quietude or conformity.*

The next article, Hillel Schmid's review of the leadership research, indicates that there are many valid styles of leadership and explores how those different styles may fit with different structures and contexts so that values and mission can best be implemented in the nonprofit sector. Organizational age, distinctive technologies, and external constituencies create different leadership demands. Sometimes leaders must be charismatic and visionary in order to create a following for a certain project. But at other times, routinized leadership that emphasizes accountability is needed for the requisite tasks to be carried out. Schmid reminds us that values and passions may find appropriate expression in bureaucracies too.

Rachel Christensen and Alnoor Ebrahim ground their examination of accountability processes in their concrete observations of how these processes unfolded in a refugee resettlement organization they studied. In the context of the resource dependency that most nonprofits experience and the sometimes counterproductive ways that some nonprofits have been known to adapt to donor demands, Christensen and Ebrahim emphasize the other side of the coin: how donors can be reminded of the organization's original purposes and their accountability processes shaped to help serve those purposes. In their vivid account of "spoon counting" in this resettlement agency, the authors shed needed light on the sorts of accountability measures that can burden the local organization with tedium in contrast to the sorts of accountability processes that can aid organizational learning and thus help the local organization to improve the value, reach, and ethics of the service it provides.

In the final article, Max Stephenson and Marcy Schnitzer examine humanitarian relief efforts: large international efforts that of necessity require the coordination of many relief organizations. In the confusing, sometimes competitive, emergency situations in which humanitarian relief organizations must do their work, Stephenson and Schnitzer show why the traditional top-down, hierarchical model of giving orders in a relief theater does not work. They suggest, in its place, a network model of semiautonomous organizations. In a networked context, preexisting organizational relationships of trust become the key to effective coordination and quick action. It is trust in the ethics and competence of other organizations that makes large relief efforts possible.

In a classic piece, David Horton Smith (1997a, 1997b) argued that the "dark matter of the nonprofit universe" was being ignored. By "dark matter" he was referring to small nonprofit organizations where many participants are volunteers and activities often are not funded by government or foundations. People participate and these entities survive only because they take on challenges that people believe in and that their members believe are not or cannot be met by for-profit or governmental institutions.

Large, bureaucratic, and centralized structures have been the undoing of many values-based undertakings.

Surely, bureaucratic templates and power-centralizing processes have been known to pressure, displace, or gut original purposes and democratic processes (DiMaggio and Powell, 1988; Leach, 2006; Milofsky, 1988; Rothschild and Whitt, 1986; Stinchcombe and Smith, 1975; Taylor, 1979; Sills, 1957). This was the main point of Michels's famous "iron law of oligarchy" (1949). But if large associations evolve toward becoming more impersonal, unethical, and guided solely by economistic value, does this mean that they started as something different—as the opposite? On this question we do not have as much research as we would like. We do not wish to romanticize small organizations since small organizations may face problems of incompetence and fraud (Cnaan, 1996), cliques that gain control and do not accept newcomers or people who are different (Wuthnow, 1994), deceptiveness about mission (Milofsky, 1997), and insufficient scope to accomplish great purposes. At the same time, we know that large, bureaucratic, and centralized structures have been the undoing of many values-based undertakings.

Although the articles in this issue address various aspects of behavior in nonprofit organizations, taken together we believe they suggest the utility of bringing our focus in the field of nonprofits back to the shared values, ethics, and passions that give rise to these organizations in the first place. Clearly, these organizations must invent or grapple with ways to accomplish their substantive purposes, while still developing the directly democratic forms of management that are often a coequal part of their original purpose. The staff and volunteers who start and join these organizations have a distinct vision of a just world, of some aspect of an ethical world, and a desire to play a personal and significant role in bringing that valued vision into being.

This means that to be true to their purpose and potential, nonprofit organizations must attend to both: their substance and their form, as their substantial purposes cannot be achieved outside of a consistent managerial form. As human values and public ethics can come to be considered and known only through a dialogic and democratic forum, we believe that organizations that are values driven raise questions and opportunities for the study of participatory methods of managing organizations. For this reason, we hope that this special issue of *NML* will encourage others who are interested in the nonprofit sector to focus on which management methods and organizational structures can best achieve substantive human values and fidelity to the images of justice that people hold dearly.

JOYCE ROTHSCHILD is professor of sociology, School of Public and International Affairs, Virginia Polytechnic Institute and State University, Blacksburg, Virginia.

CARL MILOFSKY is professor of sociology, Department of Sociology and Anthropology, Bucknell University, Lewisburg, Pennsylvania.

References

Behn, R. "The New Public Management Paradigm and the Search for Democratic Accountability." *International Public Management Journal,* 2005, *1* (2), 131–164.

Cnaan, R. A. "Confronting Crisis: When Should the Board Step In?" In M. M. Wood (ed.), *Nonprofit Boards and Leadership: Cases on Governance, Change, and Board-Staff Dynamics.* San Francisco: Jossey-Bass, 1996.

DiMaggio, P., and Powell, W. "The Iron Cage Revisited." In C. Milofsky (ed.), *Community Organizations: Studies in Resource Mobilization and Exchange.* New York: Oxford University Press, 1988.

Jeavons, T. *When the Bottom Line Is Faithfulness: Management of Christian Service Organizations.* Bloomington: Indiana University Press, 1994.

Leach, D. "The Way Is the Goal: Ideology and the Practice of Collectivist Democracy in German New Social Movements." Unpublished doctoral dissertation, University of Michigan, 2006.

Michels, R. *Political Parties: A Sociological Study of the Oligarchical Tendencies of Modern Democracy.* New York: Free Press, 1949. (Originally published in 1911.)

Milofsky, C. "Structure and Process in Community Self-Help Organizations." In C. Milofsky (ed.), *Community Organizations: Studies in Resource Mobilization and Exchange.* New York: Oxford University Press, 1988.

Milofsky, C. "Organization from Community. A Case Study of Congregational Renewal." *Nonprofit and Voluntary Sector Quarterly,* 1997, *26* (suppl.), S139–S160.

Oster, S. M. *Strategic Management for Nonprofit Organizations: Theory and Cases.* New York: Oxford University Press, 1995.

Rothschild, J. "Creating a Just and Democratic Workplace: More Engagement, Less Hierarchy." *Contemporary Sociology,* 2000, *29* (1), 195–213.

Rothschild, J., and Whitt, J. A. *The Cooperative Workplace: Potentials and Dilemmas of Organizational Democracy and Participation.* Cambridge: Cambridge University Press, 1986.

Sills, D. *The Volunteers: Means and Ends in a National Organization.* New York: Free Press, 1957.

Smith, D. H. "The Rest of the Nonprofit Sector: Grassroots Associations as the Dark Matter Ignored in the Prevailing 'Flat Earth' Maps of the Sector." *Nonprofit and Voluntary Sector Quarterly,* 1997a, *26,* 114–131.

Smith, D. H. "Grassroots Associations Are Important: Some Theory and a Review of the Impact Literature." *Nonprofit and Voluntary Sector Quarterly,* 1997b, *26,* 269–306.

Stinchcombe, A. L., and Smith, T. W. "The Homogenization of the Administrative Structure of American Industries, 1940–1970." Unpublished manuscript, National Opinion Research Center, 1975.

Taylor, R.C.R. "Free Medicine." In J. Case and R. Taylor (eds.), *Co-ops, Communes, and Collectives.* New York: Pantheon Books, 1979.

Wood, M. M. "Is Governing Board Behavior Cyclical?" *Nonprofit Management and Leadership,* 1992, *3* (2), 139–162.

Wuthnow, R. *Sharing the Journey: Support Groups and America's New Quest for Community.* New York: Free Press, 1994.

Sharing Experience, Conveying Hope
Egalitarian Relations as the Essential Method of Alcoholics Anonymous

Thomasina Borkman

The predictions of Max Weber's "iron cage" of bureaucracy and Michels's "iron law of oligarchy" failed to materialize in Alcoholics Anonymous. AA has maintained an alternative form of collectivistic-democratic voluntary organization for more than seventy years. Its organizational form was developed within its first five years and articulated in its foundational text, Alcoholics Anonymous, *published in 1939. Based on detailed histories of its early years, an analysis of AA's crucial ingredients suggests that six factors interacted to avoid the temptations of power, money, and professionalization that would have resulted in a bureaucratic form of organization or oligarchic leadership. In order to avoid death and to obtain or maintain abstinence, the desperate cofounders stumbled on the essential method: egalitarian peers share their lived experiences, conveying hope and strength to one another. In the context of the essential method, the two cofounders, from the Midwest and New York City, held similar spiritual beliefs and practiced a self-reflexive mode of social experiential learning gained from the Oxford Group, a nondenominational group that advocated healing through personal spiritual change; they downplayed their charismatic authority in favor of consulting with and abiding by the consensus of the group.*

MAX WEBER'S ANALYSIS of authority systems, a true cornerstone of modern social science, posits that the problem of succession that is faced by all charismatic associations on the death of the charismatic leader, if the association in fact continues, is the adoption of a bureaucratic form of organization (Eisenstadt,

Note: I appreciate the valuable suggestions for organizing, focusing, and improving this article from the anonymous reviewers, the editors, and Aina Stunz.

1968). Weber (1958) further predicted and lamented that additional bureaucratic features would inevitably accrue into an accumulating "iron cage," or straitjacket, that would sap flexibility and responsiveness to individuals. Weber's predictions have been seen as prescient, since many charismatic organizations do indeed become bureaucratic, and fledgling organizations that adopt some bureaucratic features often irresistibly add others. The inevitability of bureaucracy has become an assumption in social science, as has Michels's "iron law of oligarchy" (Michels, 1962), an associated idea that states that a small circle of leaders will obtain control of decision making and act to perpetuate their leadership, thereby eliminating internal democratic control.

In this article, I argue, based on a study of the structure and form of Alcoholics Anonymous (AA), that these commonly held assumptions are myths, frequently respected but often not found. Empirically, an alternative to bureaucracy not only exists but persists. An important sociological formulation of the characteristics of the egalitarian democratic alternative to bureaucracy was Rothschild-Whitt's model (1979) of the collectivist-democratic organization. The 1970s women's movement, ideologically committed to egalitarian relationships and collective decision making, created many collectivist organizations and other nonbureaucratic alternatives (Freeman, 1975; Ferguson, 1984), even though some of these became bureaucratic as they expanded to compete with established organizations in their niche due to institutional isomorphism (DiMaggio and Powell, 1983; Iannello, 1992).

Milofsky (1988) applied Rothschild-Whitt's concept of collectivist-democratic organization to community self-help organizations that are not work organizations but process-, values-, or issue-based entities relying on volunteer participation, and he contrasted them with bureaucratic organizations. In reviewing case studies on community self-help organizations, he examined the process by which formalization and the resulting decline of democracy occur in local organizations, concluding that participatory organizations face similar problematic areas of organizing that leave them open to bureaucratic solutions for expediency's sake. He concludes, "Given the difficulty of keeping small community organizations alive, it is likely that many bureaucratic organizations come about as a result of efforts to keep less structured organizations going. Rather than being a sign of moral turpitude, bureaucratization may in essence be an unintended consequence of systematic efforts by leaders to make their organizations work better" (1988, p. 210).

Early work in the study of self-help and mutual aid groups and organizations by Alfred Katz (1961) of five parents' groups whose children had mental or physical disabilities found that the majority of groups became professionalized bureaucracies within five years as the parents ceded or lost control of decision making to the professionals. Katz concluded that professionalization and bureaucratization were

The inevitability of bureaucracy has become an assumption in social science.

almost inevitable phases of the evolution of self-help groups. An updated review of self-help groups finds that there are two basic formats (Katz, 1993; Riessman and Carroll, 1995): the twelve-step anonymous group symbolized by AA, which is egalitarian and democratic, and the hierarchical nonprofit organization (those with paid staff are likely to be hierarchical self-help organizations; see Smith, 2000).

The history of AA was captured by its cofounder Bill Wilson (often referred to simply as Bill W.), who was the unofficial scribe during its early days up through the 1950s. Bill W.'s writing was semicommunal, as his drafts were reviewed and changed by the other cofounder, Dr. Robert Smith (Dr. Bob), and by members of the early groups in Akron, Cleveland, and New York City. Ernest Kurtz wrote his doctoral dissertation on a history of AA in the Department of American civilization at Harvard, which was published as *Not God* (1979) and then reissued with additional material as *AA: The Story* in 1988. William White has done extensive historical research not only on AA but on other mutual aid groups for alcoholics, reported in his book *Slaying the Dragon* (1998). In an ambitious collaborative study, eighteen authors examined AA in eight societies, showing the internationalization of the group (Makela and others, 1996). And other sociologists (for example, Maxwell, 1984; Messer, 1994; Room, 1993; Robinson and Henry, 1977; Zohar and Borkman, 1997) have dissected the practices and organizational form of AA.

Katz concluded that professionalization and bureaucratization were almost inevitable phases of the evolution of self-help groups.

These histories of AA have not questioned how and why the founding of AA was egalitarian and evolved into an internal democracy. This article contributes to the literature by examining the founding conditions, beliefs, and dispositions of the cofounders and early members, who believed that egalitarian and democratic rather than hierarchical relationships were vital to the group's effectiveness and survival.

Societal Context of AA: External Facilitating Conditions

In the social environment in which AA was founded, alcoholism was highly stigmatized as a moral failing, and public drunkenness was regarded as a crime (Conrad and Schneider, 1992). A powerful social movement, the temperance movement, had been successful in achieving the passage of the Eighteenth Amendment to the U.S. Constitution in 1919; prohibition against drinking alcohol lasted for thirteen years and had been repealed only recently when AA was founded.

At that time, no established professional or other interest group claiming to treat alcoholism stood in the way of AA's development. In fact, physicians and other health professionals rejected alcoholics. The few drying-out places extant were closing in the wake of the economic depression of the 1930s (White, 1998). These negative social conditions actually facilitated AA's development, as there were almost no alternatives for alcoholics who wanted to stop drinking. The earlier mutual aid societies for alcoholics had not lasted long or been very effective; the Washingtonians, for example, began auspiciously in the 1860s and at its peak had an estimated 600,000 pledges to abstain from drinking alcohol, but it collapsed suddenly within a year or two (White, 1998). Interestingly, AA's cofounders were aware of the Washingtonian movement's failure and patterned certain AA practices to avoid the Washingtonians' errors—such as having multiple goals (the abolition of slavery in addition to helping alcoholics to stop drinking)—but these ideas of the Washingtonian movement were applied long after AA's basic collectivist-democratic structure was established in its first five years (AA, 1991).

From its beginning, AA developed an egalitarian and nonhierarchical alternative form of organization.

A few key professionals, businessmen, and other supporters helped the fledgling fellowship with ideas and moral support but limited material support: some of the Oxford Group's ideas regarding personal spiritual change were central, while others were discarded; the psychotherapist Dr. Carl Jung's ideas about the hopelessness of alcoholism without a spiritual conversion; the psychologist William James's book that showed that spiritual conversions were experienced in a number of ways; the physician Dr. Silkworth's medical metaphor of alcoholism as a physical allergy combined with a mental obsession that assuaged guilt and created motivation for recovery, as well as Silkworth's constant moral support. Ironically perhaps, the philanthropist John D. Rockefeller Jr. made a significant contribution by refusing to give any substantial amount of money to AA, saying that money would ruin the fellowship.

Conrad and Schneider (1992) in their influential book *The Medicalization of Deviance* analyze how alcoholism in the late 1930s and 1940s was becoming defined as a disease rather than a moral failing through the efforts of the Yale Research Center of Alcohol Studies, the development of AA, and the ideas of E. M. Jellinek, early director of the Yale Center, and his associate, Mark Keller.

The Founding of AA: 1935–1939

Alcoholics Anonymous was officially born in June 1935 in Akron, Ohio, when both of its cofounders were abstinent from alcohol. From its beginning, AA developed an egalitarian and nonhierarchical alternative form of organization due to the cofounders' self-aware and deliberate work.

This analytical case study focuses on the factors that sociologically and organizationally appear to be responsible for the initial development of the organization from 1935 to 1939. These first five years were selected because in 1939 AA published its foundational text, *Alcoholics Anonymous*, describing the twelve-step program of personal recovery from alcoholism.

Cofounders Bill W. and Dr. Bob date the founding of AA from when they met in Akron, and Bill, desperately and tenuously struggling to maintain abstinence from alcohol, talked to the drunken Dr. Bob about his personal experiences with alcohol and his struggles to get and remain abstinent from drinking (Kurtz, 1979; White, 1998). When Bill arrived in Akron on a business trip in May 1935, he had experienced several of the factors that would later be regarded as critical to the founding of AA. Bill's alcoholism had progressed to the point that Dr. Silkworth at Towns Hospital, who detoxified him, regarded him as hopeless and had been ready to suggest that he be committed to an institution. Dr. Silkworth had used a medical metaphor, telling Bill that he was physically allergic to alcohol and could never drink again or he would die. But Bill had seen an old drinking buddy, Eddy B., who was now sober and who introduced him to the Oxford Group and told him of his treatment with Dr. Carl Jung, a psychotherapist in Europe. Jung told Eddy that an alcoholic was hopeless unless he had a spiritual conversion. During his last drying-out at Towns Hospital, Bill had experienced such a "conversion" and stopped drinking. He was able to understand his powerful experience in Towns Hospital as a spiritual conversion through reading the psychologist William James's book *The Varieties of Religious Experience* (1936). Bill then tried, unsuccessfully, to lecture drinking alcoholics to get them sober, but Dr. Silkworth suggested that instead of lecturing, he tell drinking alcoholics the story of his drinking, its effects, and what he was doing to stay sober.

With Dr. Bob, Bill told his story of drinking and recovery, sharing his "experience, strength, and hope" with a fellow alcoholic. The sharing and interpersonal relationship kept Bill sober and helped Dr. Bob stop drinking. This method of sharing personal experience with an experientially similar peer was viewed as the essential ingredient. The day that Dr. Bob stopped drinking is the founding date of AA: June 10, 1935.

Key Factors in AA's Choice to Be an Egalitarian Alternative to Bureaucracy

A combination of initial factors predisposed the emerging group to develop a nonbureaucratic, egalitarian organization: the essential method of AA, a distinctive co-leadership situation, significant beliefs, geographically dispersed and socially heterogeneous groups, a self-reflexive experiential learning process, and values-based (spiritual) authority—the democratic group conscience.

The Essential Method of AA: The Sharing Circle

The essential method that was "discovered" by Bill W. and Dr. Bob is the interpersonal relationship between experientially similar peers who listen to one another's experiences through telling stories about themselves. They are socially equal as peers who have experienced the same or similar situations. This equality is a central and foundational element of mutual aid as it has developed in contemporary self-help and mutual aid groups. A second element is the inherent reciprocity of the exchange—that is, the help is given to and received by both parties. A third element is that the communication is in narrative form, telling the story of one's lived experience, not analytical or abstract communication (Rappaport, 1993). A fourth element regarded as important in AA is that the alcoholic must help others to stay sober by actively communicating with and helping fellow alcoholics. What I named the "essential method" Kurtz (1979, p. 68) calls the "core therapeutic process." I have referred to this essential method as the "sharing circle"; the meaning of *sharing* is obvious, and *circle* connotes an egalitarian, nonhierarchical exchange (Borkman, 1999). The sharing circle is the foundational element of contemporary self-help and mutual aid.

> *The sharing circle is the foundational element of contemporary self-help and mutual aid.*

Riessman's influential concept of the "helper therapy" principle (1965) applies: the person helping another receives more by helping than does the recipient of the help. A primary strategy of reading literature by yourself will not keep you sober. The essential method is the egalitarian peer relationship with its mutual exchange process of telling the stories of one's experiences (see Arminen, 1998) in which I am helping you and you are helping me by listening and telling.

Distinctive Co-Leadership

The cofounders were desperate because their alcoholism was life threatening. It is significant that there were two charismatic cofounders who trusted each other, not one charismatic founder who would dominate and control. The essential method to remain sober, the sharing circle, rested on the interdependence and cooperation of the cofounders as group members, not as authority figures. They believed and were aware that the temptation to obtain power and control the group could threaten their sobriety and lead to their death. Also important was that the two leaders were to some extent opposites—Bill W. was the aggressive, extroverted entrepreneur with "grandiose visions" (White, 1998) and Dr. Bob the more cautious and considered introvert—which resulted in a balance for the evolving organization.

Significant Beliefs

Four important sets of ideas or beliefs framed the context in which Bill W. and Dr. Bob discovered the essential method of the egalitarian peers "sharing their experience, strength, and hope." The beliefs were about (1) their personality traits as alcoholics, (2) the medical metaphor of alcoholism as a disease rather than a moral failing, (3) the solution to their alcoholism (Kurtz, 1988), and (4) personal and spiritual change from the Oxford Group (White, 1998).

First, they regarded the personality traits of alcoholics as self-destructive and totally self-centered; alcoholics were in effect "playing God" by engaging in "self-will run riot" and defying authority. Kurtz named his impressive history *Not God*, as he thought this concept lies at the heart of the AA fellowship and program (1979).

Second, Dr. Silkworth, who detoxified Bill W. at Towns Hospital before Bill met Dr. Bob in Akron, presented Bill with a medical metaphor, telling him that he was physically allergic with a mental obsession of alcohol and could never drink again or he would die. Silkworth's ideas were an early unscientifically substantiated version of the disease concept of alcoholism, which replaced the temperance movement's and others' beliefs of alcoholism as moral degeneracy.

Third, the solution to chronic drunkenness had four aspects as interpreted by Kurtz (1988): "*Utterly hopeless, totally deflated, requiring conversion, and needing others,* the drinking alcoholic was quite obviously not perfect, not absolute, not God" (p. 35). Alcoholics were regarded at that time by the medical community and by Bill W.'s and Dr. Bob's own experiences as hopeless. But how could the self-centered and willful alcoholic stop drinking and maintain sobriety? He had to be totally deflated (in AA's terms, "hitting bottom") by recognizing that he was not perfect, "not God," and had a spiritual conversion in which he understood that the solution to imperfection was interdependence with others, especially his experientially similar peers.

From the beginning, social diversity in worldviews was inherent among the founding members.

Fourth, both Bill W. and Dr. Bob had independently been involved with the Oxford Group before they met in Akron, and the early meetings of what became AA were held in conjunction with the Oxford Group in New York (with Bill W.) and in Akron (with Dr. Bob) for several years. Founded in the early 1900s by Frank Buchman, a Lutheran minister from Pennsylvania, the Oxford Group was a nondenominational spiritual group that followed some principles of early Christianity. "The central idea of the Oxford Group was that the problems of the world could be healed through a movement of personal spiritual change. This change came about through a set of core ideas and practices for daily living" (White, 1998, p. 128). These core ideas and practices (including self-awareness, confession, conversion, restitution, and sharing through witness) were developed and adapted by the cofounders and early groups to be part of the twelve steps, the program for individual recovery as articulated by AA by 1939.

Geographical Dispersion and Social Heterogeneity

The cofounders lived in different geographical areas—Dr. Bob in the Midwest and Bill W. in New York City—and the groups led by each cofounder developed slightly different ideas and practices. From the beginning, social diversity in worldviews was inherent among the founding members. For example, the New York group included members who were atheists, whereas the Akron group had a number of devout Protestants. The unity of the larger group was viewed as critical to the survival of the individuals because of their life-threatening disease and the interdependent methodology to remain abstinent. Thus, the cofounders and their local groups communicated frequently with one another and developed respectful and egalitarian ways to resolve conflicts and accommodate the diversity and differences of opinion.

Self-Reflexive Experiential Learning Process

The cofounders learned and used a self-reflexive experiential learning process (see Borkman, 1999) of becoming aware of negative behavior and attitudes, admitting their faults, and making restitution for them through their association with the Oxford Group and their practice of the essential method. The cofounders and early members understood that unless their negative character traits were dampened, they could not stay sober. The self-reflexive spiritual learning process of the Oxford Group was an antidote to their negative tendencies. Self-reflection could lead to personality changes that would help maintain their abstinence. These principles, which they adapted to fit the personality traits and behavior of alcoholics, were important parts of what became known as the twelve steps—the principles for living a spiritually based life that would keep them sober (White, 1998; Kurtz, 1979).

As the initial groups developed in Akron and New York, the members realized that alcoholics' distrust of hierarchical authority combined with their defiant attitudes meant that the manner in which they were introduced to ideas about getting and staying sober had to be carefully thought out. Lectures, rules, and requirements would be rejected. New members responded positively to the method and authority of the sharing circle (the experiential knowledge of stories of one's recovery experiences) and to suggestions rather than requirements. The approach that Bill W. had used to reach Dr. Bob was used to shape the way that principles for individual recovery were communicated.

Values-Based (Spiritual) Authority: The Democratic Group Conscience

Although the cofounders led the fledgling groups in terms of major visions and ideas, they always consulted the group members about any significant issue regarding personal recovery or the group process. From the beginning, the group, not the cofounders, evolved as the major authority, and the consensus (not a mere majority) of the group became the norm; they called this the *group conscience*. Bill W.'s grandiose schemes and visions (White, 1998) were squelched time and again by group consensus, and Bill submitted to their authority. The cofounders did not behave as conventional charismatic leaders who control and dominate their organization, but consistently involved group members in making decisions. These events illustrate how the process of self-reflection and learning from experience led to a principle that became institutionalized as a meta-rule: members shall be active in their own governance as they are active in their sobriety.

The Rejection of Money, Professionalization, and Hierarchy

The six factors for an egalitarian democratic organization just described could yet be derailed when the cofounders and fledgling groups faced the temptations of power, prestige, professionalization, and money, which often lead to bureaucracy and oligarchy.

From 1936 to 1938, Bill W. was tempted by money, power, and professionalization. Heavily in debt, Bill and his wife, Lois, devoted their time to helping alcoholics while living on Lois's meager income from a sales job. In 1937 the Towns Hospital proprietor asked Bill to professionalize the hospital's services for detoxifying alcoholics. Bill was tempted but took the idea back to the New York AA group, which rejected the idea (White, 1998). The wealthy John D. Rockefeller Jr. was asked to contribute fifty thousand dollars to the struggling organization, but he declined, saying most decisively that money would ruin AA's valuable fellowship (White, 1998). However, Rockefeller did provide a modest weekly sum of thirty dollars to both Bill and Dr. Bob so they could work full time to build AA.

This formative insight by an outsider was initially disappointing to Bill but not to the New York group. Bill later understood the wisdom of avoiding the dangers of extensive accumulation of money. Relying on members' donations to keep the groups self-supporting helped them to focus on the primary goal of helping alcoholics to achieve sobriety (Cheever, 2004). Without substantial financial resources, the professionalization of work with paid staff responsible for administering the organization became a moot issue; AA groups would be maintained on contributed volunteer labor, which would also reinforce their recovery. Smith (2000) argues that a critical dividing line is reached when paid staff take over administration, changing the dynamics and structures of grassroots associations.

In 1938, Bill, still financially insolvent and occupied with grand visions, set up the Alcoholic Foundation in order to obtain tax-deductible charitable gifts from wealthy philanthropists and expand AA through education, treatment, and other programs (Kurtz, 1979). Five trustees—three nonalcoholics, Dr. Bob, and an alcoholic from the New York group—were to convince benefactors that their money would be well spent. A second company, Works Publishing, was formed to issue stock to raise money to finance the publication of their forthcoming book, *Alcoholics Anonymous*. (In 1940 the Alcoholic Foundation took over Works Publishing so that the foundation was the sole owner of the book.) The book sold few copies until AA received media publicity in 1941. Proceeds from book sales were used to pay rent for the foundation's office in New York, associated expenses, and postage and to provide information to the public, AA groups, and potential members; no person profited financially.

> *Smith (2000) argues that a critical dividing line is reached when paid staff take over administration, changing the dynamics and structures of grassroots associations.*

Despite the original charter, the Alcoholic Foundation was not a governing unit of AA in any sense. Managed by Bill W., it acted more as a legal repository of copyrights, a service unit that housed and sold AA's book and maintained an address where the public could send letters or that AA groups could contact for information or help with group issues. Bill applied the same experiential learning approach to issues of group functioning that was used in the twelve steps of personal recovery. Thus, the Alcoholic Foundation was not used to centralize control, which remained in the group conscience of the grassroots groups.

> *In 1950 the cofounders established the General Services Conference, which was and remains the sole policymaking and decision-making body on the national level.*

Was AA a Collectivist-Democratic Organization by 1939?

By 1939, when the publication of the book *Alcoholics Anonymous* established the suggested program of recovery, the fledging fellowship had three local and unincorporated independent groups (Akron, Cleveland, and New York) and the incorporated Alcoholic Foundation that acted as a service, not a governing, unit. It had successfully and self-knowingly forgone the temptations of money, power, and professionalization. Was AA then operating as a collectivistic-democratic organization as described by Rothschild-Whitt (1979) and Rothschild and Leach (2006)?

Rothschild-Whitt developed her formulation of collectivistic-democratic organizations on the basis of economic worker cooperatives rather than voluntary mutual aid membership associations such as AA. She identified eight dimensions of governance and structure that distinguished the ideal typical collectivistic-democratic organization from the equivalent bureaucracy. Table 1 presents a preliminary analysis of AA in 1939 in relation to these eight dimensions. Note that where workers and employment are assumed because she was studying economic worker cooperatives, we are substituting roles that were established for maintaining the local group or the Alcoholic Foundation. On all eight dimensions, AA was similar to the collectivist-democratic organization.

The Maturation of AA: Leadership Succession

We telescope the story during the middle years from 1940 to 1950 when the cofounders established and institutionalized a democratic structure on the national level (still extant today) and underwent the succession of leadership by formally turning over the governance of AA to the groups in 1955 (White, 1998).

In effect, the transfer of leadership from the cofounders to the membership occurred at AA's national conference in July 1950, just months before Dr. Bob died (AA, 1980). In 1950 the cofounders established the General Services Conference, which was and remains

Table 1. Comparison of the Organizational Dimensions of AA in 1939 with Rothschild-Whitt's (1979) Ideal Typical Dimensions of Collectivist-Democratic Organizations

Dimension	Collectivist-Democratic Organization	AA in 1939
Authority	Resides in collective as a whole	Group conscience; Alcoholic Foundation servant to local groups
Rules	Minimal stipulated rules; ad hoc individual decisions	Almost no rules; suggested procedures such as the twelve steps
Social control	Primarily personal or moral appeals; select homogeneous personnel	Only personal and moral appeals; voluntary self-defined membership
Social relations	Holistic, personal, of value as such	Holistic, personal, intrinsically valued
Recruitment and advancement	Employment based on friends, values, personality, and informally assessed skills and knowledge; no hierarchy of jobs	Roles to maintain group based on length of sobriety, personality, values; roles not hierarchical
Incentive structure	Normative and solidarity incentives primary; material ones secondary	Normative, solidarity, and self-interest incentives; no material ones
Social stratification	Egalitarian; if any reward differentials, collective limits them	Egalitarian; seasoned sobriety has more influence than newcomers
Differentiation	Minimal division of labor; demystify expertise; interchangeable roles	Minimal division of labor; all roles simple and interchangeable

the sole policymaking and decision-making body on the national level. It is described in AA's *Service Manual* (AA, 1984–1985). Beginning with representatives elected from local groups to districts, then regions, and then to the state level, a general service representative from each state is elected to attend the conference (with additional representatives from states with large numbers of AA members). Each April, the unincorporated conference deliberates on any issues needing attention for AA as a whole or the national-level service bodies. The conference charter states that it is to be "the guardian of the world services and the Twelve Steps and Twelve Traditions of Alcoholics Anonymous. The Conference shall be a service body only; never a government for Alcoholics Anonymous" (AA, 1984–1985, p. 23). The legally incorporated nonprofit entities at the national level were set up as services, not as governing bodies dictating to local groups, district committees, or regional bodies.

When asked in 1955 why AA needed the conference, Bernard Smith, chairman of the board of trustees (and a nonalcoholic) who had participated in the charter's development, answered: "We need it because we, more than all others, are conscious of the devastating effect of the human urge for power and prestige which we must insure can never invade A.A. We need it to insure A.A. against government, while insulating it against anarchy; we need it to protect A.A. against disintegration while preventing over integration. We need it so that Alcoholics Anonymous, and Alcoholics Anonymous alone, is the ultimate repository of its Twelve Steps, its Twelve Traditions, and all of its services" (AA, 1984–1985, p. 33).

Smith's statement shows an awareness of the potentially devastating effects of individual power and prestige, oligarchy, or its reverse, anarchy. This awareness is part of the self-reflexivity that is openly discussed and was present from the beginning because of the practices and ideas AA inherited from the Oxford Group.

AA has had two incorporated nonprofit organizations: AA Grapevine, which publishes the magazine for and by members, and AA World Services (originally called the Alcoholic Foundation when established in 1938), which handles other publications and services to local groups and the public. A General Service Board whose slates of potential members are approved or disapproved by the conference are the trustees of the two corporations (AA, 1984–1985). Thus, the local groups, through their elected representatives to the conference, make policy and decisions for the two national-level incorporated service organizations. The local unincorporated groups, through their elected representatives to the conference, make policy for and direct the affairs of the General Service Board. A pictorial representation shows an inverted pyramid in which the thousands of local groups direct the two incorporated service organizations at the national level.

The cofounders applied the same method and authority to developing principles for group functioning as they did for individual recovery: experiential knowledge and wisdom of the collective. Bill W. collected principles and suggestions from the variety of groups he and Lois visited or heard from by letter or telephone; these evolved into the Twelve Traditions for group functioning in the 1950s (AA, 1957, 1991).

Conclusion

A number of organizational and sociological analysts characterize AA as currently having a decentralized, cell-like organizational structure. Robin Room (1993), a sociologist and expert in alcohol studies, summarizes some of the major indicators that AA is egalitarian, nonhierarchical, and nonbureaucratic:

> Membership is defined inclusively: on the other hand, the stance to the outside world is isolationist, neither accepting nor seeking outside influence. Power resides at the base, in the "group conscience" of the face-to-face group; all superstructures are defined as responsible to the base-group level. Forms of relation are egalitarian, both within the group and between groups. Thus group officers and delegates are elected by group members, and incumbency is expected to rotate between members. Groups are autonomous, and cannot be subject to control either by other groups or by some superior body. The problem of where assets are held is solved in large part by a prohibition on owning property or holding substantial assets. . . . To an unprecedented extent,

AA has succeeded in creating an organization that breaks Michels' "iron law of oligarchy" (1962) by building in structures and principles that minimize the professionalization of leadership and keep effective organizational power at the level of egalitarian face-to-face interaction [p. 171].

The basic organizational unit of AA is the local group, which is unincorporated and relatively autonomous from other groups as well as from the national-level service structure (Room, 1993; Zohar and Borkman, 1997). There are no exclusive territories or franchises; an established group cannot prevent a new group from forming nearby. Groups cannot own property or obtain money except by members' donations so that conflict and power seeking because of property or extensive resources are limited. Similarly, groups cannot affiliate with or endorse hospitals, treatment centers, or any other organization or institution, thus minimizing opportunities for conflict and competition. Membership is open to anyone "who has a desire to stop drinking," and groups neither keep membership lists nor require membership dues. Interestingly, there is no mechanism or sanction for ousting a person from the self-defined membership. Internally, groups have equality and democracy: leadership is elected and rotating, decision making is open and by consensus, and external anonymity is maintained. No professional relationships are allowed (which could compromise the equality of internal membership by having a professional-client relationship within the group).

Alcoholics Anonymous is so well known in the United States as a twelve-step self-help/mutual aid group for recovering alcoholics that it is part of the popular culture. Less well known is the fact that AA is the model for perhaps a hundred other twelve-step anonymous groups (Madara, 1999) and that twelve-step anonymous groups probably constitute one-third of all self-help groups in the United States (Wuthnow, 1994).

AA originated in the 1930s in middle-class North America, but in successive stages it has been able to outgrow the cultural milieu of its birth. In 1990, it had an estimated membership of 2 million worldwide. AA began as a mutual-help movement aiming at inner reform and addressing the existential problems of a small minority. Its organizational principles outline strict limits against any attempts to effect political change or carry out cultural propaganda. Nevertheless, the end result is that important segments of the general public in North America are deeply affected by the twelve-step program (Makela and others, 1996).

While AA eschews any involvement in politics, alcohol treatment, or any issue external to the organization, paradoxically it has had major influences, albeit indirectly, on American culture (Bloomfield, 1994; Room, 1992; White, 1998). The idea of alcoholism as a disease, not a moral failing, has been extensively promulgated and accepted in American society due partly to AA's indirect influence (Conrad and

Alcoholics Anonymous is so well known in the United States as a twelve-step self-help/mutual aid group for recovering alcoholics that it is part of the popular culture.

Schneider, 1992). The majority of substance abuse treatment centers in the United States use many ideas from AA and send their clients to AA meetings in the community (McCrady and Miller, 1993). The single most popular model of professional alcohol and drug treatment, termed the Minnesota Model, was initially developed as about half AA ideas and half professional ones (Anderson, McGovern, and DuPont, 1999; Spicer, 1993); the Minnesota Model has subsequently been exported to Europe and other countries (Makela and others, 1996). Ideas of recovery that evolved from AA members and their twelve-step practices have spread to other areas of society, including mental health (Room, 1992).

> *[AA] has successfully resisted professionaliza-tion, bureaucracy, and the concentration of power for more than seventy years.*

While successful as a voluntary, nonprofessional, mutual help alternative to professionalized substance abuse treatment, AA also has its share of critics. Some people reject the disease concept (Fingarette, 1988). Some people with drinking problems reject its religious-appearing ideas and concept of higher power; others view it as a cult, dislike its emphasis on abstinence from alcohol, or criticize it for other reasons. Other mutual help groups such as Rational Recovery, Women for Sobriety, Secular Organizations for Sobriety, and Moderation Management have been established in reaction against AA (see review by Humphreys, 2004).

This analytical case study of AA shows that during its first five years (1935–1939), the two charismatic cofounders and early members laid the collectivist-democratic foundation of AA, rejecting Weber's concept of bureaucracy. During its maturation period with the issue of leadership succession, the two cofounders voluntarily relinquished all control of AA in 1955, giving the power and control to the entire membership in all the local groups, not to a small oligarchy of leaders or to a bureaucratic hierarchy with trustees. Alcoholics Anonymous did not follow the predictions of Weber's iron cage or of Michels's iron law of oligarchy because it has successfully resisted professionalization, bureaucracy, and the concentration of power for more than seventy years.

The cofounders and early AA members were desperate late-stage alcoholics, near death, who recognized that if they did not follow the essential method that resulted in sobriety, they would not survive. The motivation to create the collectivistic-egalitarian ingredients of group governance seems to have been the fear of their death and interest in helping fellow alcoholics. Importantly, the measures they took to ensure their sobriety as well as their interest in helping other alcoholics resulted in principles of group functioning that were collectivistic-democratic and institutionalized in AA by 1955. Thus, what was beneficial for sobriety and the health of the individual was also effective for the maintenance of a collectivistic-democratic organization. These conditions are unlikely to characterize many new organizations. AA may be unique.

AA provides a model of how an organization can grow to a very large size, reaching millions of people, yet retain its decentralized, egalitarian, cell-like organizational structure. It illustrates the power and efficacy of a democratic group process that supports human dignity and equality. In the words of the eighteen authors who studied AA internationally in eight societies, "Alcoholics Anonymous (AA) is one of the great success stories of our century" (Makela and others, 1996, p. 3).

THOMASINA BORKMAN *is professor of sociology at George Mason University and past president of the Association for Research on Nonprofit Organizations and Voluntary Action.*

References

Alcoholics Anonymous. *Alcoholics Anonymous: The Story of How Many Thousands of Men and Women Have Recovered.* New York: Works Publishing, 1939.

Alcoholics Anonymous. *Alcoholics Anonymous Comes of Age: A Brief History of A.A.* New York: Alcoholics Anonymous World Services, 1957.

Alcoholics Anonymous. *Dr. Bob and the Good Oldtimers.* New York: Alcoholics Anonymous World Services, 1980.

Alcoholics Anonymous. *The A.A. Service Manual Combined with the Twelve Concepts for World Service [1962].* New York: Alcoholics Anonymous World Services, 1984–1985. (Originally published in 1969.)

Alcoholics Anonymous. *Twelve Steps and Twelve Traditions.* New York: Alcoholics Anonymous World Services, 1991. (Originally published in 1953.)

Anderson, D. J., McGovern, J. P., and DuPont, R. L. "The Origins of the Minnesota Model of Addiction Treatment—A First Person Account." *Journal of Addictive Diseases,* 1999, *18,* 107–114.

Arminen, I. *Therapeutic Interaction: A Study of Mutual Help in the Meetings of Alcoholics Anonymous.* Helsinki: Finnish Foundation for Alcohol Studies, 1998.

Bloomfield, K. "Beyond Sobriety: The Cultural Significance of Alcoholics Anonymous as a Social Movement." *Nonprofit and Voluntary Sector Quarterly,* 1994, *23* (1), 21–40.

Borkman, T. *Understanding Self-Help/Mutual Aid: Experiential Learning in the Commons.* New Brunswick, N.J.: Rutgers University Press, 1999.

Cheever, S. *My Name Is Bill: Bill Wilson—His Life and the Creation of Alcoholics Anonymous.* New York: Simon & Schuster, 2004.

Conrad, P., and Schneider, J. W. *Deviance and Medicalization: From Badness to Sickness.* Philadelphia: Temple University Press, 1992. (Originally published in 1980.)

DiMaggio, P., and Powell, W. W. "The Iron Cage Revisited: Institutional Isomorphism and Collective Rationality in Organizational Fields." *American Sociological Review,* 1983, *48,* 147–160.

Eisenstadt, S. N. (ed.). *Max Weber on Charisma and Institution Building: Selected Papers.* Chicago: University of Chicago Press, 1968.

Ferguson, K. *The Feminist Case Against Bureaucracy.* Philadelphia: Temple University Press, 1984.

Fingarette, H. *Heavy Drinking: The Myth of Alcoholism as a Disease.* Berkeley: University of California Press, 1988.

Freeman, J. *The Politics of Women's Liberation.* New York: Longman, 1975.

Humphreys, K. *Circles of Recovery: Self-Help Organizations for Addictions.* Cambridge: Cambridge University Press, 2004.

Iannello, K. P. *Decisions Without Hierarchy: Feminist Interventions in Organization Theory and Practice.* New York: Routledge, 1992.

James, W. *Varieties of Religious Experience.* New York: Modern Library, 1936.

Katz, A. H. *Parents of the Handicapped.* Springfield, Ill.: Thomas, 1961.

Katz, A. H. *Self-Help in America: A Social Movement Perspective.* Old Tappan, N.J.: Twayne, 1993.

Kurtz, E. *Not God: A History of Alcoholics Anonymous.* Center City, Minn.: Hazelden, 1979.

Kurtz, E. *A.A.: The Story. A Revised Edition of Not-God: A History of Alcoholics Anonymous.* San Francisco: HarperSanFrancisco, 1988.

Madara, E. "Self-Help Groups: Options for Support, Education, and Advocacy." In P. G. O'Brien, W. Z. Kennedy, and K. A. Ballard (eds.), *Psychiatric Nursing: An Integration of Theory and Practice.* New York: McGraw-Hill, 1999.

Makela, K., and others. *Alcoholics Anonymous as a Mutual-Help Movement: A Study in Eight Societies.* Madison: University of Wisconsin Press, 1996.

Maxwell, M. A. *The Alcoholics Anonymous Experience: A Close-Up View for Professionals.* New York: McGraw-Hill, 1984.

McCrady, B. S., and Miller, W. R. (eds.). *Research on Alcoholics Anonymous: Opportunities and Alternatives.* New Brunswick, N.J.: Rutgers Center of Alcohol Studies, 1993.

Messer, J. G. "Emergent Organization as a Practical Strategy: Executing Trustee Functions in Alcoholics Anonymous." *Nonprofit and Voluntary Sector Quarterly,* 1994, 23 (4), 293–307.

Michels, R. *Political Parties: A Sociological Study of the Oligarchical Tendencies of Modern Democracy.* New York: Free Press, 1962. (Originally published in 1911.)

Milofsky, C. (ed). *Community Organizations: Studies in Resource Mobilization and Exchange.* New York: Oxford University Press, 1988.

Rappaport, J. "Narrative Studies, Personal Stories, and Identity Transformation in the Mutual Help Context." *Journal of Applied Behavioral Science,* 1993, 29 (2), 239–256.

Riessman, F. "The 'Helper Therapy' Principle." *Social Work,* 1965, 10(2), 27–32.

Riessman, F., and Carroll, D. *Redefining Self-Help: Policy and Practice.* San Francisco: Jossey-Bass, 1995.

Robinson, D., and Henry, S. *Self-Help and Health: Mutual Aid for Modern Problems*. London: Martin Robertson, 1977.

Room, R. "Healing Ourselves and Our Planet: The Emergence and Nature of a Generalized Twelve-Step Consciousness." *Contemporary Drug Problems*, 1992, *19*, 717–740.

Room, R. "Alcoholics Anonymous as a Social Movement." In B. S. McCrady and W. R. Miller (eds.), *Research on Alcoholics Anonymous: Opportunities and Alternatives*. New Brunswick, N.J.: Rutgers Center of Alcohol Studies, 1993.

Rothschild, J., and Leach, D. "Avoid, Talk or Fight: Alternative Cultural Strategies in the Battle Against Oligarchy in Collectivist-Democratic Organizations." In R. Cnaan and C. Milofsky (eds.), *Handbook of Community Movements and Local Organizations*. New York: Springer, 2006.

Rothschild-Whitt, J. "The Collectivist Organization: An Alternative to Rational-Bureaucratic Models." *American Sociological Review*, 1979, *44*, 509–527.

Smith, D. H. *Grassroots Associations*. Thousand Oaks, Calif.: Sage, 2000.

Spicer, J. *The Minnesota Model: The Evolution of the Multidisciplinary Approach to Addiction Recovery*. Center City, Minn.: Hazelden Foundation, 1993.

Weber, M. *The Protestant Ethic and the Spirit of Capitalism*. New York: Scribner, 1958.

White, W. L. *Slaying the Dragon: The History of Addiction Treatment and Recovery in America*. Bloomington, Ill.: Chestnut Health Publications, 1998.

Wuthnow, R. *Sharing the Journey: Support Groups and America's New Quest for Community*. New York: Free Press, 1994.

Zohar, A., and Borkman, T. "Emergent Order and Self-Organization: A Case Study of Alcoholics Anonymous." *Nonprofit and Voluntary Sector Quarterly*, 1997, *26* (4), 527–552.

For bulk reprints of this article, please call (201) 748-8789.

Nonprofit Management & Leadership   DOI: 10.1002/nml

The Ironic Value of Loyalty
Dispute Resolution Strategies in Worker Cooperatives and Conventional Organizations

Elizabeth A. Hoffmann

Employee retention and satisfaction are key concerns for employers. In this article, I explore a variety of worker characteristics that affect how workers respond to troubling events and circumstances in the workplace. I examine how they approach their workplace problems, focusing on the value of their loyalty and how this loyalty might affect their problem-related decisions. This research suggests that worker loyalty presents an irony for managers, which I call the ironic value of loyalty: workers with greater loyalty are less likely to exit when they encounter workplace problems, decreasing turnover problems, yet when more loyal workers choose to remain at work, they are more likely to raise grievances, either formally or informally, to confront the problems. Thus, worker loyalty appears both to solve and create problems for managers dealing with worker discontent.

EMPLOYERS AND MANAGERS are often concerned with both employee turnover and employee grievances. This article addresses both of these concerns. Drawing on qualitative data, this study provides insights into why some employees stay and why others leave when they encounter workplace problems. It also presents what I call the ironic value of loyalty: workers with greater loyalty will stay when they encounter problems, yet they are more likely to voice disgruntlement when these problems need to be addressed. Thus, managers and employers facing the ironic value of loyalty want

Note: I thank Bob Perrucci, John Stahura, Joyce Rothschild, and Glenn Muschert for their comments on earlier drafts and Mark C. Suchman, Lauren Edelman, Jane Collins, and Howard Erlanger for their help and encouragement at earlier stages of this project. This research was supported by a National Science Foundation grant (SBR-9801948). This article is based on an earlier version published in *Social Forces* (June 2006) by the University of North Carolina Press. Used by permission of the publisher.

greater loyalty because it brings greater employee retention, but then must contend with the more loyal and more vocal employees who are willing to speak out on behalf of their own and other workers' problems. Moreover, employees who are particularly committed to the organization's ideological cause may be more likely to exit over what might appear to be minor difficulties if those employees interpret those difficulties as the organization's failure to fulfill its ideological commitment.

This article builds on earlier research on workplace dispute resolution to explore this irony. Using data from three industries, I explore how some workers complain, how others stay and remain quiet and passive in the face of workplace problems, how others stay yet come forward with their problems, and how others leave altogether. I argue that workers' feelings of loyalty account for at least some of these differences.

Theoretical Background: Loyalty, Workplace Disputes, and Worker Cooperatives

The core strength of nonprofit organizations is the people they employ.

The core strength of nonprofit organizations is the people they employ. Often these workers join nonprofits because of commitment to a broader agenda, goal, or ethic of which the organization is a part. As such, employees often enter nonprofit workplaces with a heightened awareness of the values and ethics, implied or explicit, in their own jobs and in their employing organization.

In discussions of workers' values and ethics in both nonprofit and for-profit businesses, loyalty is often a key concept. How organizations treat their workers may affect which values and ethics the workers demonstrate within the organizations. Cooperatives, being worker owned, often treat workers better than similar private businesses and, some argue, also enjoy greater worker loyalty. Loyalty may have a direct impact not simply on workers' sentiments but on what actions they take at work.

In confronting workplace problems, people's two courses of action are to (1) leave the organization, that is, exit, or (2) stay and express their displeasure, that is, voice. Whereas both exit and voice behaviors can send a similar message to the organization, causing it to improve, voice is the more difficult option for workers (Hirschman, 1970). When the exit option is unavailable, the only way dissatisfied people can communicate their dissatisfaction is with voice, so that, as Hirschman explains, "the role of voice would increase as the opportunities for exit decline" (p. 34). Thus, in situations where one cannot exit or the cost of exit is particularly high (such as membership in one's family, state, or church), the voice option is the only way to express displeasure. In addition, dissatisfied people could instead engage in "acquiescence," meaning that they would remain "dumbly faithful" to the firm without leaving or voicing their discontent (Hirschman, 1970, p. 31). In this article, I operationalize acquiescence as the category "toleration," meaning that the problem is perceived but no action is taken.

When both exit and voice are options, the decision to exit or remain will be affected by how effective voice would be. If workers "are sufficiently convinced that voice will be effective, then they may well postpone exit" (Hirschman, 1970, p. 37). Other research, such as that on whistle-blowers, demonstrates that sometimes workers go outside their organization and whistle-blow only after their voices have been ignored by the supervisors they turned to (Rothschild and Miethe, 1999). This supports Hirschman's argument that exit is closely linked to voice.

But when will people stay and fight, and when will they cut bait and leave? Loyalty may be the important factor that shapes whether people will exit or voice (Hirschman, 1970). Those with greater loyalty are more likely to stay and try to change the organization from within. This is particularly true if they believe that their efforts have the power to influence the organization (Hodson, 2001).

In addition, even workers without great loyalty might force themselves to stay and voice—that is, resist the exit option—if their membership in the organization was achieved with substantial difficulty. For example, workers might not exit if positions at the desired workplace were only infrequently available or if, in order to achieve and maintain the position, they must successfully complete a rigorous training and probationary period. These hard-won positions might be more difficult for workers to exit without exhausting the options for voice. Thus, entry costs further heighten the likelihood of choosing voice rather than exit, since those who have endured difficulty in joining the organization will be less likely to discard their membership lightly (Hirschman, 1970).

Some research suggests that members of worker cooperatives—businesses that are comanaged and co-owned by their workers—will have greater loyalty than workers in conventional businesses (for example, Cornforth, Thomas, Lewis, and Spear, 1988; Rothschild and Whitt, 1986). Members of worker cooperatives often have ideological attachments to their workplace. Sometimes they specifically sought jobs in the cooperatives; other times they simply happened on these jobs but then became converted to the cooperative workplace ideology. Moreover, some worker cooperatives require that their members pay an amount of money to buy into the cooperative before they may begin working. Thus, members of worker cooperatives—whether because of self-selection reasons or factors created by the structure of these businesses—may have greater loyalty. The flip side of this greater loyalty is that members of worker cooperatives may also have higher expectations for the organization to which they have entrusted their loyalty, thereby increasing the probability of greater dissatisfaction (Rothschild and Whitt, 1986).

To investigate the impact of loyalty on the dispute resolution strategies of exit and voice, I compare conventional organizations and

Members of worker cooperatives may also have higher expectations for the organization to which they have entrusted their loyalty.

collectively run organizations. I examine three very different industries, comparing one conventional and one cooperative business in each. Contrasts in loyalty between the conventional and cooperative organizations are explored to determine the significance for workers' subjective experiences and workplace conduct. After establishing that people in cooperatives have greater loyalty, I compare how these differences in loyalty between the cooperatives and conventional businesses affect their workers' dispute resolution behaviors.

I show here that members of worker cooperatives express more loyalty to their organization. I also establish the ironic value of loyalty: these workers were more likely to include voice as a way they anticipate resolving workplace problems, yet in most cases they were also likely to steadfastly remain with the organization, even as they disagreed with how the organization was being run. In contrast, the workers in conventional businesses were less likely to express much loyalty to their organization and also were less likely to anticipate using voice to resolve workplace problems. In addition, workers who experienced high entry or exit costs—those in the coal mining industry—were especially unlikely to consider leaving the company as a way to resolve problems, regardless of levels of loyalty.

Sampling and Methods

One of the key benefits of qualitative studies is the high validity possible: the researcher can understand the greater context, obtain a large overview, and triangulate the accounts of differently situated interviewees with various bases of knowledge. In gathering data for this study, I conducted interviews; observed behavior; read related documents and articles; attended companies' business meetings and, when possible, grievance hearings; and participated in aspects of some businesses.

Sample

I conducted 128 interviews: 18 at HealthBite Distributors, 35 at Organix Coop, 14 at Private Taxi, 20 at Coop Cab, and 41 at Coal Cooperative/Valley Colliery. (Coal Cooperative and Valley Colliery were the same physical mine, but under different ownership and management systems, as explained below.) For each site, Table 1 provides summary statistics on the interviewees as well as on the organizations themselves. I did not identify a specific group of workers whom I knew to have had disputes, but spoke to all interviewees about their workplace experiences generally. I included a wide variety of interviewees to maximize the range of problems and experiences as well as the variety of solutions and expectations to be included in this study.

The interviewees were drawn from six work sites in three industries: coal mining, taxicab driving, and organic food distribution. The industries ranged from the coal mining industry, where the workers are very pro-union, to the nonconformist or loner-oriented taxicab

Table 1. Summary of Sites and Interviewees

	Industry	Type of Organization	Location	Number of Workers	Number Interviewed
Valley Colliery	Coal mine	Conventional	Wales (United Kingdom)	252	38[a] (15%)
Coal Cooperative	Coal mine	Worker cooperative	Wales (United Kingdom)	239	41[a] (17%)
Private Taxi	Taxicab driving	Conventional	Wisconsin (United States)	120	14 (12%)
Coop Cab	Taxicab driving	Worker cooperative	Wisconsin (United States)	150	20 (13%)
HealthBite Distributors	Organic food	Conventional	London (United Kingdom)	32	18 (56%)
Organix Coop	Organic food	Worker cooperative	Halifax (United Kingdom)	50	35 (70%)

[a]These two businesses are the same site but at different times: Valley Colliery = before employee buyout; Coal Cooperative = after buyout, as worker cooperative. The Coal Cooperative totals include two men and one woman who had not worked at the coal mine before the worker buyout.

industry and the progressively oriented organic food industry. The industries also ranged from having a predominantly male workplace culture, such as coal mining, to being less explicitly gendered, such as the organic food industry. These differences in workplace culture are somewhat reflected in the industries' different gender balances: fifty-to-one men to women at the coal mines, five-to-one in taxi driving, and one-to-one in organic food. Table 1 summarizes the organizational attributes of each business.

All businesses in this study met several key criteria. First, the company needed to have a formal system for grievance resolution. Second, it had to be sufficiently large that a formal grievance system was necessary. For this study, the minimum size of an organization was thirty workers. Third, each business had to be a stable organization with established procedures; none was less than two years old. Fourth, no organization could be part of a larger organization. In addition, each cooperative included in the study had to be a true worker cooperative, with all employees being equal shareholders and no outside shareholders—not merely an Employee Stock Option Plan (ESOP) company.

Within each industry, I compared a worker cooperative (nonhierarchical workplace in which all workers are comanagers and co-owners) to a conventional, hierarchical business matched in size and gender ratios. The coal mining and organic food distribution were studied in the United Kingdom, and the taxicab industry was studied in the United States. Because these two cultures are sufficiently similar, no cross-cultural comparison is included in this study. Admittedly, people are more class conscious in the United Kingdom, but the fundamental disputing culture, as seen in the two legal systems, is sufficiently similar (Wheeler, Klaas, and Rojot, 1994).

Each cooperative included in the study had to be a true worker cooperative, with all employees being equal shareholders and no outside shareholders.

Worker cooperatives are in some ways a midpoint between conventional businesses and nonprofit organizations in that cooperatives do not fully forget about profits, yet they still maintain a strong social contract with their workers. Cooperatives endeavor to accumulate money for their worker-owners as both profit and salary. In this sense, worker cooperatives are aware of profits. However, unlike most conventional businesses, cooperatives need not be profit maximizing. Most decision making in worker cooperatives involves other values in addition to concerns about profit, such as worker participation, empowerment, and democracy. Often these values compete strongly with, and sometimes supersede, the concern over profit making, creating workplaces that often resemble the multigoal complexities of many nonprofit organizations.

The businesses are summarized in Table 1. I looked at two organic food distributors: Organix Coop, a worker cooperative located in the mid-north of England, and HealthBite, a conventional business located near London. While some workers in the industry described the attraction of these jobs as simply the need for a paycheck, others spoke of their dedication to the organic and whole food movement and saw their jobs as a type of activism. Organix Coop was begun more than twenty years ago by progressive college students who wanted to create a better, healthier, more egalitarian work environment. This consciousness of the worker cooperative ideology still permeates the business. Workers at Organix Coop became members after completing a probationary period and being voted into membership by the current members. Once they became members, they received their part of the company's profits, as well as wages, and became vested in the company, with each worker owning a single share of stock, regardless of tenure. If they left the cooperative, they had to sell their share back to the company, generating a type of severance pay.

Both the conventional taxicab company (Private Taxi) and the cooperative taxicab company (Coop Cab) are located in the same midwestern U.S. town. Coop Cab was begun more than twenty years ago by cab drivers who were out of work due to strikes at two of the city's main taxicab companies. It embraced the worker cooperative ideology in trying to create a better workplace, although not as strongly, uniformly, or dogmatically as Organix Coop. Workers at the cooperative, Coop Cab, became members once they had successfully completed a probationary period as determined by the membership committee. Once members, they shared in the profits of the company, in addition to their wages, although they did not receive individual shares that could be sold back when leaving the company.

Finally, Valley Colliery and Coal Cooperative were deep-pit mines, meaning deep underground mining as opposed to strip mining. The two coal mines in this study were actually the same physical mine under two different systems of ownership and management. All interviews for both were conducted several years after the reopening of the mine as a cooperative. The alias "Valley Colliery" refers to this mine when it was nationally owned by the British Coal Board, and "Coal Cooperative" refers to the mine once it became a worker cooperative. The mine was the last deep pit in Wales and one of the few left in the United Kingdom. As such, employment at the mine—both when it was part of British Coal and after it became a worker cooperative—held important cultural significance for the miners, who deeply identified with the mining occupation. During the period between the closing of the mine by the Coal Board and its reopening as a cooperative, some out-of-work miners took factory jobs, the only other jobs in the area. They described them with much contempt, often saying that they would rather go on government assistance than work there again. Once the mine was reopened as a cooperative, workers had to become members before they could begin work at the mine. In order to participate, each worker had to buy a single share of the cooperative at approximately thirteen thousand dollars. As with the organic food cooperative, this share entitled the member to profit sharing as well as wages. When the worker left the co-op, this share would be bought back by the company.

Employment at the mine . . . held important cultural significance for the miners, who deeply identified with the mining occupation.

Data Collection

In conducting this study, I employed a qualitative comparative case method to study three very different industries, each with one cooperative and one conventional organization. In gathering data, I interviewed workers; observed behavior; read related documents and articles; attended companies' business meetings and, when possible, grievance hearings; and participated in aspects of some businesses (went down into the coal pit, rode along in the taxicabs).

The interviews ranged from twenty minutes to over five hours, with most lasting between thirty and ninety minutes. Interviewees were asked mostly general, open-ended questions, but with some direct questions, especially as follow-up inquiries. In discussing grievance resolution strategies respondents often drew on examples from their experience. All interviews were tape-recorded and transcribed, so all quotations used here are direct. These data were coded and analyzed using the qualitative data software NVivo. Some of these themes were responses to explicit questions (for example, "In what ways is your job difficult?"). However, many others were extracted from the responses of interviewees to broader questions (for example: "How would you describe your job?" "How would you recommend/criticize your job to another worker in the same industry?" "What would you change about your job if you could just snap your fingers and it would be different?") or to follow-up questions to other responses. Thus, many codes, such as "loyalty," were not the result of a direct question or set of questions intended to measure loyalty, but were produced by careful analysis of interviewees' responses to various questions.

Nonprofit Management & Leadership   DOI: 10.1002/nml

Results and Discussion

One key voice mechanism employees use when dealing with problems at work is grievance raising (Hirschman, 1970). In this article, I focus on how this specific voice mechanism of grievance raising works differently in organizations with greater and less workplace loyalty. I operationalize "grievance raising" as bringing forward both formal and informal grievances and define strikes as a type of formal grievance.

After assessing that worker cooperative members truly did hold greater loyalty to their organization than did their counterparts in conventional organizations, I compared how these two groups of workers addressed workplace problems. They mentioned three dispute resolution strategies: raising a grievance ("voice"), learning to cope with the problem (what I call "toleration," a rough equivalent of Hirschman's "acquiescence"), and quitting their job altogether ("exit"). Although exit and toleration are not actually ways to resolve disputes, they are strategies workers use to end the conflict in their work lives.

The worker cooperative members consistently made statements about their loyalty to the organization. The conventional business employees spoke infrequently about loyalty.

Loyalty

I did not simply assume that members of worker cooperatives would have greater loyalty to their organizations, although the literature strongly indicated this. Rather, I compared the statements of the worker cooperative members with those of employees in the other conventional businesses. The worker cooperative members consistently made statements about their loyalty to the organization (92 percent). The conventional business employees spoke infrequently about loyalty and when they did express such sentiments, they spoke of loyalty to the industry as a whole. For example, a member of the taxicab co-op described a high level of loyalty to the cooperative, which many other co-op members echoed:

> Yet they choose to stick with [Coop Cab] because they believe in the cooperative and they feel a loyalty to the cooperative. I think there's something that's very good about that . . . because they believe that the way the coops are structured is a lot more beneficial to the workers. And the coops tend to deal with issues that help the community and they're more community-oriented than profit-making. So having a loyalty to that motivation is, in my mind, a better motivation than going someplace where your wages might be higher, but you're not necessarily supporting something that's community-oriented, community-based.

This loyalty was not found in the sentiments of peer workers employed by matched conventional businesses. For example, one worker from HealthBite provides a concise, if dramatic, articulation of the sentiment of being simply a hired hand: "If you have a problem, good luck! We've got a complaint procedure we go to if we got a complaint about something or anything like that. They *try* and solve it. But, really, we're on our own." Although the conventional business employees did mention loyalty to the goals of the industry (such as HealthBite workers' commitment to organic and whole foods), these workers generally did not mention loyalty to the organization or to coworkers.

Voice and Loyalty

The absence of organizational loyalty among these conventional-organization employees made them less likely to include voice in their dispute resolution strategies. In contrast, the presence of loyalty made the worker cooperative members more likely to anticipate engaging in voice. Comparing each percentage within each industry, the cooperative members are more likely to engage in dispute resolution (how this article is operationalizing voice) than their same-industry conventional counterparts, as Table 2 shows.

Table 3 presents the frequencies of the employees in each type of organization, showing how many expressed loyalty and how many in each category indicated voice, toleration, or exit. The table

Table 2. Percentages of Employees Who Mentioned Each Dispute Resolution Strategy

	Taxicab Industry		Whole Foods Industry		Coal Mining Industry	
	Private Taxi	Coop Cab	HealthBite Distributors	Organix Coop	Valley Colliery	Coal Cooperative
Voice	57%	100%	56%	91%	90%	100%
Toleration	36	5	61	29	11	2
Exit	36	20	17	23	0	0

Note: Percentages sum to greater than 100 percent in some cases because the categories are not exclusive; some interviewees mentioned more than one dispute resolution strategy. There is no "no response" category. All interviewees provided at least one strategy (voice, toleration, or exit).

Table 3. Frequencies of Loyal and Not Loyal Employees Who Mentioned Each Dispute Resolution Strategy

	Taxicab Industry				Whole Foods Industry				Coal Mining Industry			
	Hierarchical		Cooperative		Hierarchical		Cooperative		Hierarchical		Cooperative	
	Loyal	Not Loyal	Loyal	Not Loyal	Loyal	Not Loyal	Loyal	Not Loyal	Loyal	Not Loyal	Loyal	Not Loyal
Voice	5	3	18	2	6	4	31	1	32	2	41	0
Toleration	0	5	0	1	1	10	7	3	2	2	1	0
Exit	0	5	0	4	0	3	7	1	0	0	0	0

Note: These frequencies are of the number of statements made and total to greater than the number of interviewees because several interviewees described more than one dispute resolution strategy.

presents only the raw numbers, rather than the percentages, to enable readers to make comparisons across the table. Table 3 clearly demonstrates that workers who expressed loyalty were more likely to engage in voice than workers who did not express loyalty and that cooperatives were more likely to have members who expressed loyalty.

Taxicab Industry. The members of Coop Cab were much more likely (100 percent) to describe a type of voice (formal or informal grievances) when explaining their dispute resolution strategies, in contrast to those in Private Taxi, who less frequently mentioned voice strategies (57 percent). For example, one woman from Coop Cab explained that sometimes one had to speak up and bring a grievance if a decision happened that harmed the cooperative in some way: "I felt that [the worker manager] had really screwed up. . . . [That policy decision] totally went against what a cooperative should do. Now, I could have just left it at that. . . . In a way, it wasn't going to really affect me. But I had a duty to say something [and bring a grievance]. . . . Just as [the worker manager] is a co-owner, I'm a co-owner and it's my coop, too." This woman believed that sometimes one must bring a grievance, even if one did not experience that harm directly to oneself.

> *This woman believed that sometimes one must bring a grievance, even if one did not experience that harm directly to oneself.*

In contrast, workers at Private Taxi were more likely to take a more informal route when they tried to resolve their grievances. A Private Taxi driver explained that people try whatever means they can, with whomever they can, when they attempt to resolve grievances informally:

> Everyone goes to whoever they think they're gonna get some satisfaction from. If someone has a good relationship with [the owner], then they'll probably go to [him] and see what they can do. If someone has a good relationship with [the manager], at this point in time, they'll go to [him] to see what they can do. In some cases, people will go to the dispatcher and say, "Hey, you know, listen, I got this problem with this guy that's doing this other shift, and I feel like he's screwed me over." Or whatever.

Given this pattern, it is not surprising that Private Taxi employees were more likely to have toleration among their dispute resolution strategies (36 percent as opposed to Coop Cab's 5 percent).

Organic Food Industry. Workers at Organix Coop talked about how they had heard about the worker cooperative from friends and intentionally sought out Organix because they wanted a cooperative work environment. Some said they had left more highly paid jobs in the private sector to take a job at Organix to be part of a cooperative. In contrast, HealthBite workers often described their motivation for their job at HealthBite as focusing on their paycheck. Although some were motivated by a commitment to the organics movement, others saw their jobs simply as an easily accessible, low-skill job that provided a decent wage. Most stumbled into their current jobs through word-of-mouth or through answering ads in the newspaper.

Worker cooperative members were much more likely (91 percent) to mention voice (formal or informal grievances) as one of their dispute resolution strategies than their counterparts in the conventional organic food company (56 percent). Thus, the employees at HealthBite were less likely (56 percent) to attempt to resolve their workplace problems, but when they did, they were more likely to rely on resolving grievances informally (not reflected in Table 2, but see Hoffmann, 2003, for a discussion of formal versus informal dispute resolution in the taxicab industry).

Understandably given the voice pattern above, toleration strategies were more frequently mentioned by workers at HealthBite (61 percent) than at Organix Coop (29 percent). A representative employee at HealthBite explained that often his preferred path is to do nothing: "If someone else isn't doing their work and I'm doing it all, what I've learned in the past, is to just shut your mouth and keep doing it. 'Cause that's how it works. I just shut up and keep doing it." These employees had developed various ways to cope with problems they could not or would not resolve. Their ability to tolerate allowed them to avoid any sort of grievance resolution and yet remain in their jobs.

Both the voice and toleration patterns in the organic food industry clearly support Hirschman's model. The exit patterns do not follow the basic exit-voice framework but do support Hirschman's broader thesis, as I discuss below. In the organic food industry, a somewhat higher percentage of worker cooperative members mentioned quitting their jobs as a way to resolve workplace problems (23 percent) than did their counterparts in the conventional company (17 percent).

Workers at HealthBite who mentioned exit as a strategy felt that quitting was an easy option if they found themselves unhappy at their jobs because such jobs are easily replaced and therefore quite disposable. However, workers at Organix Coop explained that they would quit if they felt betrayed by the cooperative, not because they could find another similar job easily.

Thus, although the percentages (23 percent at Organix Coop; 17 percent at HealthBite) do not reflect the classic ironic value of loyalty with regard to exit, the reasons for exit still support this theory. Previous research has noted that "those [workers] who care the *most* about the quality of the product and who, therefore, are those who would be the most active, reliable, and creative agents of voice are, for that very reason, also those who are apparently likely to exit first in cases of deterioration" (Hirschman, 1970, p. 47). Therefore, it is interesting to note that Organix Coop, the co-op with the greatest cooperative ideology zeal, is also the co-op where its members report more exit strategies. Indeed, the anticipated use of exit by the Organix Coop members in the event of frustration with or betrayal

Organix Coop, the co-op with the greatest cooperative ideology zeal, is also the co-op where its members report more exit strategies.

by the cooperative offers an interesting twist on the ironic value of loyalty in that it is these people, who most care about the organization as a concept, who are also more likely to consider exit.

Coal Industry. The percentages of various interviewee responses within the coal industry offer the least support for Hirschman's thesis in some ways. Yet in other ways the industry acts much as Hirschman would predict. Here, the percentages of workers who mentioned raising a grievance either formally or informally (voice) was very similar for both the cooperative (100 percent) and the conventional business (90 percent). Despite this numerical similarity, the range of topics that workers could raise was much greater in the cooperative. One electrician, for example, recounted a formal grievance brought soon after the mine reopened as a cooperative: a grievance about the toilet paper: "Another thing they wanted changed when we came back as a cooperative was the toilet paper. The toilet paper [the miners used], they were the old government bloody thick paper. A simple thing like that. And the managers, under British Coal, their toilets up there, they had the soft, bloody soft, pink paper. The things like that. Silly little things. But it matters. It says, 'I'm no better than that manager over there and he's no better than me.'" For this miner, raising this grievance, despite its somewhat trivial focus, was important; it demonstrated loyalty to his cooperative's ideal of equality among all members.

In addition, the variation between the company's workers regarding mentioning toleration as a strategy does support Hirschman's framework. Workers at Valley Colliery were five times more likely to mention developing coping mechanisms as a way for dealing with problems at work as compared to those at Coal Cooperative.

The number of workers who mentioned leaving as one of their dispute resolution strategies (exit) was identical: none. No one at either Coal Cooperative or Valley Colliery mentioned quitting as a possible way to resolve workplace grievances. This could be tied to the workers' expressed concern in preserving their jobs and keeping the mine open, since many deep-pit mines in the United Kingdom had already been closed. These miners expressed concern not with simply keeping a job, but with keeping these jobs. Many of them had fathers and grandfathers who had been deep-pit coal miners. For them, deep-pit mining was part of their identity and their heritage. "[In] these communities here, probably [for] anybody [who] works in [Valley Colliery], either their father or grandfather or great-grandfather, uncle or great uncle, was constantly working [in the coal industry]. They been brought up not only on coal mining when they are in the mine, but probably the conversation at their home has been about coal mining and in the pub on Saturday, and the club on Saturday, are predominantly coal talk. . . . We come from a coal culture."

Because these workers saw the jobs at the coal mines as precious commodities, it is not surprising that no one mentioned leaving. Indeed, the workers at both of the coal mines—Valley Colliery and

Coal Cooperative—so strongly identify with their particular mine that to leave that organization would mean having to change their identity, to reconceptualize who they are. Thus, the exit costs are extremely high for both groups of miners, resulting in no one considering exit as a possible dispute resolution strategy.

In addition, miners who were forced to take factory jobs (the only other jobs available) between the time of the mine closing and its reopening as a cooperative detested the factory work. They stated that they would rather have no job than to have to return to factory work. This factory work was small-scale assembly of computer parts—what more than one miner referred to as "dainty women's work." In many ways, the only way to maintain their identity, particularly their masculine identity (see Cheng, 1996; Connell, 1995), was to work in the mines.

Moreover, the mining co-op also had the highest entry costs, demanding a thirteen-thousand-dollar buy-in by each worker. Therefore, one might speculate that the members of the cooperative would be even more reluctant than their conventional organization counterparts to exit, although one cannot have a rate lower than zero to actually express this.

Conclusion

These data show some support for the classic ironic value of loyalty and Hirschman's exit-voice framework. This has important significance for workers' subjective experiences and workplace conduct, particularly in the nonprofit sectors. Employees in nonprofit jobs may be more likely to have come to their positions with certain ideological goals in mind. Indeed, some employees may even actively seek out jobs specifically within certain nonprofit sectors as a demonstration of their ideological commitment. Similar to the workers in cooperatives, these nonprofit organization employees might enter and embrace their jobs with a higher level of loyalty, yet might also hold their organizations to higher ideological standards.

The data demonstrate that workers with greater organizational loyalty are more likely to use voice when confronted with workplace problems. This means that workers who are very loyal to the organization are more likely to raise issues and actively confront problems they perceive in their workplace. While constructive criticism and concern from committed workers will enhance the organization, managers and employers should not be disheartened or surprised by this. Although this raising of informal and formal grievances by loyal employees might cause disruptions to the organization, this feedback, if addressed correctly, can improve the organization.

However, when workers' ideological loyalty surpasses their organizational loyalty and when these two loyalties are in conflict, even members with high loyalty might resort to exit. The data discussed here illustrate this with the situation of a cooperative that no longer

Employees in nonprofit jobs may be more likely to have come to their positions with certain ideological goals in mind.

meets its egalitarian goals, and therefore its most ideologically loyal employees become more likely to exit. This situation is also a concern for the nonprofit sector, where employees perceive the organization as no longer fulfilling its ideological promises or falling short of its goals in whatever industry it operates.

Thus, this article provides some concrete insights for managers and employers in nonprofit organizations. The findings imply that simply creating or finding employees with a high level of loyalty is not sufficient to ensure low turnover. In addition, nonprofit companies that use motivational techniques to pull employee support behind the organization's ideological goals (in order to increase productivity, heighten commitment, and so on) may actually experience greater exit than companies that simply try to generate high employee enthusiasm for the company itself. Thus, the ironic value of loyalty suggests that the nonprofit with the greatest employee loyalty to its cause might experience the greatest employee disruption: through both protest exits and formal and informal grievances.

> *The other employment options that are available to workers will have an impact on their dispute resolution strategies.*

This article's findings also imply that high exit costs, such as those found in the coal industry, will affect not only the decision to exit but also the decision to voice. Thus, managers and employers of nonprofit organizations should assess how valuable their positions are to their employees. To what degree do the employees consider working at a particular nonprofit organization a rare opportunity or just a paycheck?

On a practical level, this underscores that no company or industry can be examined in isolation. The other employment options that are available to workers will have an impact on their dispute resolution strategies. If unemployment rates are high or the available job alternatives are unattractive, workers may be disinclined to choose exit.

Future research should explore how employees might attempt radical reform in organizations by using a whistle-blowing form of voice. By holding greater loyalty to their industry or to an ethic than they may hold to their organization, some employees might embrace whistle-blowing grievances. In doing so, they might significantly alter some organizations' objectionable yet customary practices and thereby significantly alter how both their own organization and their industry do business.

ELIZABETH A. HOFFMANN is an assistant professor of sociology at Purdue University, West Lafayette, Indiana. Her research explores legal consciousness and workplace dispute resolution.

References

Cheng, C. *Masculinities in Organizations.* Thousand Oaks, Calif.: Sage, 1996.

Connell, R. W. *Masculinities.* Berkeley: University of California Press, 1995.

Cornforth, C., Thomas, A., Lewis, J., and Spear, R. *Developing Successful Worker Co-operatives.* Thousand Oaks, Calif.: Sage, 1988.

Hirschman, A. O. *Exit, Voice, and Loyalty: Responses to Declines in Firms, Organizations, and States.* Cambridge, Mass.: Harvard University Press, 1970.

Hodson, R. *Dignity at Work.* Cambridge: Cambridge University Press, 2001.

Hoffmann, E. A. "Legal Consciousness and Dispute Resolution: Different Disputing Behavior at Two Similar Taxicab Companies." *Law and Social Inquiry,* 2003, *28,* 691–715.

Rothschild, J., and Miethe, T. D. "Whistle-Blower Disclosures and Management Retaliation: The Battle to Control Information About Organization Corruption." *Work and Occupations,* 1999, *26,* 107–128.

Rothschild, J., and Whitt, J. A. *The Cooperative Workplace: Potentials and Dilemmas of Organizational Democracy and Participation.* Cambridge: Cambridge University Press, 1986.

Wheeler, H. N., Klaas, B. S., and Rojot, J. "Justice at Work: An International Comparison." *Annals of the American Academy of Political and Social Science,* 1994, *536* (1), 31–42.

For bulk reprints of this article, please call (201) 748-8789.

Nonprofit Management & Leadership   DOI: 10.1002/nml

Leadership Styles and Leadership Change in Human and Community Service Organizations

Hillel Schmid

This article describes and analyzes leadership styles and leadership change in human and community service organizations. Based on the assumption that leadership styles must adapt to changing environments, four case studies of human and community service organizations are presented in an effort to determine the appropriate leadership style for each of the organizations described at different stages of the organizational life cycle. Emphasis is placed on the need to adapt leadership styles to the unique circumstances that prevail in the organization, based on a theoretical model that integrates different perspectives on leadership roles. The main argument is that in order to be effective, leaders must develop awareness of and sensitivity to changing situations and organizational constraints. Specifically, they should know when to adopt a task-oriented style versus a people-oriented style and when to adopt an internal versus an external orientation.

THE LITERATURE ON LEADERSHIP in political, governmental, public, commercial, industrial, social, and community organizations dates back to the early 1900s and covers a wide range of areas. Almost every conceivable dimension of the topic has been explored, including various perspectives of the concept of leadership, sources and roots of leadership, leadership traits, functions of leaders, and the impact of environments on leadership roles, as well as task-oriented versus people-oriented leadership, among other issues.

In this article, I present and analyze different types of leadership and patterns of management in human and community service organizations. My specific aims are to (1) describe, analyze, and evaluate changing situations in organizations, and learn how different leadership styles fit those situations and contingencies at different stages

NONPROFIT MANAGEMENT & LEADERSHIP, vol. 17, no. 2, Winter 2006 © 2006 Wiley Periodicals, Inc.
Published online in Wiley InterScience (www.interscience.wiley.com). DOI: 10.1002/nml.142

of the organizational life cycle; (2) shed light on the range of leadership styles and how they fit different organizational structures; and (3) help public boards of nonprofit and community organizations select leaders who are suited to the organization's unique characteristics and culture, in accordance with the organization's stage of development in the organizational life cycle.

Leadership in the Twentieth Century: Theoretical Approaches and Research Findings

A historical review of the theoretical and empirical literature dealing with the concept of leadership reveals a variety of approaches that have developed over the years. One of the first approaches, which prevailed in the literature from 1930 to 1950, was the traits approach (Bargal, 2001; Hersey and Blanchard, 1982). This approach focused on personal attributes of leaders, assuming that leaders are born rather than made. However, the attempts to identify leadership traits were not successful, and this approach was rejected later.

Subsequent studies revealed that leadership is a dynamic concept that involves processes of constant change in the leaders themselves, their followers, and the situations that they encounter (Hemphill, 1949). These studies focused on the leadership approach, but never developed a solid theoretical framework to explain their findings (House and Aditya, 1997).

In the late 1940s and early 1950s, research on leadership began to emphasize patterns of behavior and leadership styles (Likert, 1961; Stogdill and Coons, 1957). Two concepts that prevailed in the literature during that period were employee orientation and production orientation. To a great extent, the two orientations are parallel to the autocratic (task) and democratic (relationship) patterns, as well as to "initiating structure" and "consideration," a term used by Halpin (1959) to refer to the human relations aspect of leadership.

The next major developments in research on leadership took place in the 1970s with the introduction of contingency theories: Fiedler's contingency theory of leadership (Fiedler, 1967, 1977), the path-goal theory of leadership effectiveness (House, 1971; House and Mitchell, 1974), life cycle theory (Hersey and Blanchard, 1982), cognitive resource theory (Fiedler and Garcia, 1987), and decision process theory (Vroom and Yetton, 1973). All of these theories attempted to link leadership patterns with different types of organizational and personal situations or contingencies.

Those approaches reflect a major transition from the traits approach to new theoretical models that emphasize the impact of changing organizational situations on patterns of leadership and claim that leaders need to adapt their leadership patterns and management styles to the demands of the organization's situation. These approaches also led to the development of other leadership theories. For example, the theory of charismatic leadership derived from the path-goal theory (House, 1977), and cognitive resource theory derived from contingency theory.

Later paradigms and theories, which are known as neocharismatic theories, were developed in the mid-1970s. These include the theory of charismatic leadership (House, 1977), theory of transformational leadership (Bass, 1985; Burns, 1978), attributional theory of charismatic leadership (Conger and Kanungo, 1987), visionary theories (Bennis and Nanus, 1985; Nanus, 1992), and the value-based theory of leadership (House, Shane, and Herold, 1996), which is an extended version of House's theory of charismatic leadership (House, 1977).

Based on these theoretical approaches and as a conceptual framework for the organizational analysis presented in this article, I propose a perspective that views the leader of an organization as creating a vision. According to that perspective, vision is defined as the capacity to create and communicate a compelling picture of a desired state of affairs, impart clarity to this vision, and induce commitment to it (Bennis and Nanus, 1985). According to Bennis and Nanus, "The critical point is that the vision articulates a view of a realistic, credible, attractive future for the organization, a condition that is better in some important ways than what now exists" (p. 89). Consistent with that view, however, we argue that it is not enough for a leader to create a vision. The real test of a leader is whether he or she can transmit that vision to followers, articulate it to them clearly, and mobilize their support. Moreover, the role of the leader is to cope with the challenges, opportunities, risks, and constraints of the organizational environment. In this context, the leader's function is to create supportive environments that will provide the legitimation necessary for the organization to achieve its desired goals.

The leader's function is to create supportive environments that will provide the legitimation necessary for the organization to achieve its desired goals.

Another dimension I address is that of the leader's relationship with his or her followers. Clearly, the leader will have difficulty achieving the desired goals without cooperation from staff members. In this connection, House and Baetz (1979) propose a definition stating that "an action by a group member becomes an act of leadership when the act is perceived by another member of the group as an acceptable attempt to influence that person or more members of that group" (p. 345). According to that perspective, an act of leadership is considered an interaction between the leader and a group of people with whom and for whom he or she works. Therefore, the leader needs to exhibit empathy and consideration and to actively engage in intellectual stimulation of followers. Toward that end, leaders attempt to influence their followers' thought and imagination, beliefs, and values by teaching them to conceptualize, contemplate, and cope with abstract contents, thereby heightening their capacity for problem awareness and problem solving. This behavior characterizes the transformational leader, who treats followers in an individualized way that caters to their emotional and personal needs and promotes their growth and fulfillment (Dvir, Eden, Avolio, and Shamir, 2002).

Regarding the internal orientation, where leaders focus on ongoing maintenance of the organization, we adopted the concept of the transactional leader proposed by Bass (1985). The transactional leader is characterized as the agent at workplaces and organizations who assigns tasks to employees, delivers rewards, and promises rewards for further efforts. This type of leader sets goals, clarifies desired outcomes, provides feedback, and exchanges rewards for accomplishments.

Based on these assumptions, I propose an approach that argues that leaders are not selected, trained, and evaluated solely according to their personality traits, but according to the extent to which their qualities fit different and changing organizational situations. I assume that leaders operate in different organizations and should therefore follow organizational and behavioral models that enable them to assess and analyze needs in a given situation and adapt their style and pattern of leadership accordingly. In that way, they will be able to achieve organizational effectiveness, which will allow them to realize the vision of the organization and attain desired outcomes.

> *It can be argued that leaders shape patterns of organizational and structural behavior in accordance with their personal characteristics and in keeping with their style of leading the organization.*

The assumption underlying this article is that because organizations vary in their ideologies, goals, objectives, organizational cultures, and core activities, as well as in the characteristics of their human resources, levels of professional expertise, and psychological and professional maturity, they will behave differently in their choice of leaders. In a similar vein, it can be argued that leaders shape patterns of organizational and structural behavior in accordance with their personal characteristics and in keeping with their style of leading the organization. Thus, members of the organization need to adapt themselves to the leader's vision, demands, and expectations, as well as to the leader's strategies for attaining goals. If there is a conflict between the demands and contingencies faced by the organization and the pattern of leadership, or if the leaders' demands and expectations conflict with the behavior and expectations of their followers, the organization may encounter difficulties that prevent it from achieving its declared goals.

I also assume that across the organizational life cycle there is a need for different types of leaders with different qualities that suit the specific stage of the organization's development. Here, too, if the patterns of leadership are not suited to the organization's stage of development, there may be a crisis that undermines the workers' confidence in the management, impedes the functioning of the organization, reduces the efficiency of the organization's performance, and prevents the attainment of organizational effectiveness.

Against this background, I present case studies of four types of human service organizations and evaluate their organizational properties and specific needs at different stages of the organizational life cycle. In so doing, I identify the types of leadership that are most appropriate for predicting the success of these organizations in attaining their goals and adapting to changing environments.

First, I present case descriptions of the four types of human service and community organizations. Then, based on the literature review and the four case studies, I propose a theoretical model for analyzing and evaluating the extent to which different patterns of leadership are suitable for different organizational and structural situations.

Types of Human Service and Community Service Organizations: The Case Studies

The descriptions of the four types of organizations that provide human and community services are based on longitudinal studies dealing with organizational behavior, structure, management, and strategic behavior in these organizations.

The first organization is the community service organization, which provides social services according to age groups and areas of specialization. With regard to age groups, the community service organization offers programs for clients of different ages, from infants to senior citizens. The organization operates in an environment characterized by a high level of uncertainty in terms of available resources. To ensure that the activities meet a high standard of quality, the organization has to compete with other neighborhood and governmental organizations for essential scarce resources.

Studies on the relationship between variables such as extent of decentralization in decision making among executives and perceived autonomy among workers, on the one hand, and several organizational variables that typify community service organizations, such as coordination of activities and control over the quality of programs, on the other hand, have revealed interesting findings (Schmid, 1992a, 1992b). The extent of perceived decentralization among executives and the extent of perceived autonomy among workers correlated positively and significantly with the other structural variables examined. Clear positive correlations were also found between perceived autonomy among workers and perceived decentralization among executive directors. Similarly, perceived autonomy among program directors correlated positively with their perceived impact on decision making and program implementation. Moreover, positive correlations were found between perceived autonomy, perceived coordination, and perceived control among executive directors as well as among program directors. Regarding the effect of those selected variables (worker autonomy, decentralization of authority and powers, coordination, and control) on organizational effectiveness, the findings have revealed that decentralization of authority is the most significant variable (Schmid, 1992a, 1992b).

The second type of organization includes residential boarding institutions for disadvantaged children and institutions for people with retardation. These settings are closer to the definition of closed systems or total institutions, which function according to a specific

Perceived autonomy among program directors [of community service organizations] correlated positively with their perceived impact on decision making and program implementation.

set of laws and codes. In those institutions, therapeutic staff work together with other professionals who develop special relationships with the residents. The professional staff members largely determine the children's lifestyle and daily routine, make decisions for them, and mediate with the external environment. There are specific regulations regarding activities, rights and obligations, curriculum, leisure time, social activities, dress code, and time schedules. Control and monitoring mechanisms are applied in all areas of organizational life, and workers acknowledge the authority of the executive director. In this connection, a study on the relationships between different organizational and structural properties that influence the administrative style of the directors in those institutions has revealed several interesting results. First, the directors and staff perceived the level of formalization in those settings to be high. Level of formalization and extent of coordination were found to have the strongest influence on perceived autonomy among the professional and administrative staff as well as on satisfaction among residents (Schmid and Bar-Nir, 2001). It was also found that the combination of a high formalization level, close coordination and supervision, and limited autonomy for the staff are conditions for attainment of organizational effectiveness and satisfaction among staff members and residents.

A third type of organization, the home care organization, provides an array of services that may be brought into a home singularly or in combination to assist people with chronic illness and frail elderly people who are highly dependent on others. In this type of organization, service technologies are relatively simple, and the home care worker has a direct relationship with elderly clients who are dependent on others for assistance. The staff of home care organizations consist mainly of women with relatively low levels of education and professional training, whose opportunities for professional advancement are limited. Turnover rates in home care organizations are high due to considerable burnout and low salaries. Despite repeated attempts to introduce and establish advanced methods of supervision and monitoring, this area has turned out to be one of the main weaknesses of home care organizations. Hence, there is a risk that the workers will attempt to compensate for their low salary and poor working conditions by deliberately cutting back on the amount, scope, and quality of services.

A longitudinal study of home care organizations revealed several factors that affect the patterns of leadership and management style of their executive directors (Schmid and Nirel, 1995). First, the workers expect to be treated fairly, and the more they perceive their treatment as fair, the higher their level of satisfaction as well as their assessments of the organization's performance and outcomes. Similarly, the more training the workers receive and the better their working conditions, the higher their assessments of the organization's performance. Another finding revealed a positive correlation between control and workers' assessments of organizational performance.

The fourth type of organization includes those that provide services for children and youth at risk. The main services provided by these organizations are afternoon drop-in centers, counseling and guidance, social and extracurricular activities, legal advice, hot lines, and hostels, as well as services that aim at socialization to new values, advocacy, and promotion of children's rights. Although most of these organizations are established by private entrepreneurs, their funding sources are diverse. A large share of their revenue (47 percent) derives from government and public budgets, 37 percent derives from foundations and private donors, and a small share (7 percent) derives from fees paid for services (Schmid and others, 2001). Studies indicate that paid employees and volunteer staff enjoy a high level of autonomy. Although the workers express a high level of satisfaction and are willing to work beyond their official hours, they also indicate that they feel burdened by a heavy workload.

A study that examined organizational, structural, and managerial patterns in organizations for children at risk revealed several interesting findings (Schmid and others, 2001). One significant finding relates to the high level of perceived autonomy reported by executives and workers alike. In addition, strong positive correlations were found between perceived workload, autonomy, and job satisfaction. The interaction between those variables was found to have a strong impact on attainment of organizational effectiveness (see also Bargal and Guterman, 1996), and autonomy had an especially significant impact on achievement of effectiveness. Findings have also shown that autonomy and job satisfaction generate a high level of commitment to the organization's goals and clients (see also Kendall and Knapp, 1995; Mirvis, 1992).

Autonomy and job satisfaction generate a high level of commitment to the organization's goals and clients.

A Theoretical Model

Based on the literature review and the case studies, I propose a theoretical model for analysis of the relationships between types of leadership and types of human and community service organizations. The model consists of two main axes that, to my understanding, are central to leadership roles and function. One axis relates to the extent of the leader's task orientation versus people orientation. At one end is task orientation, which relates to the leader's emphasis on planning, organization, implementation, budgeting, administrative communication, coordination, decision making, and functions that are perceived as instrumental aspects of the leader's role and enable him to focus on goal achievement with minimal consideration of the human factor. At the other end is people orientation, which relates to the leader's emphasis on functions such as motivating workers, training and development, listening and empathy, interpersonal communication, building the administrative team, trust, and establishing stable human relations. These are the expressive aspects of the leader's role, including the leader's body language and facial expressions, which convey the leader's expectations of their followers and reflect the relationships that develop between them.

The second axis, defined as "internal versus external orientation," expresses the importance of the external environment in influencing the organizational and structural behavior of social service organizations versus the leader's orientation to the organization's internal affairs. This axis plays an important role in setting priorities for the leader's work. Specifically, in the attempt to maintain the organization's internal stability and achieve maximal effectiveness through standardization of processes, the leader needs to focus on managing external environments that have become more competitive, control resources, and have a major impact on the organization. Thus, the external environment gains considerable power in relation to the organizations. As Aldrich and Pfeffer (1976) aptly stated, "Administrators manage their environments as well as their organizations, and the former activity may be as important or more important than the latter" (p. 83). In a situation of stiff competition for scarce resources, if organizations fail to channel efforts toward raising the funds they need for their activities or fail to change hostile environments into supportive environments, they are likely to face crises that will undermine their stability.

Figure 1 displays four quadrants, which combine the two axes. The quadrants will be used to analyze existing and potential patterns of leadership in the four case studies described above.

If organizations fail to channel efforts toward raising the funds they need . . . or fail to change hostile environments into supportive environments, they are likely to face crises.

Discussion and Analysis

In this section, I use the four quadrants in Figure 1 as a basis for examining the patterns of leadership that are most suitable in each of the four case studies.

In the case of residential boarding institutions, it appears that the most appropriate leadership pattern is characterized by a high level of centralized authority, with extensive use of formal powers and very little staff participation (quadrant I). This type of leader fits the profile of the transactional leader, which is appropriate for maintaining the organizational system and ensuring that workers are duly rewarded for their tasks. Executives in these settings have to make sure that the professional level of workers and services remains adequate and that any changes introduced in processes and programs are moderate, slow, and gradual. Thus, the leader's behavior tends to be formalistic and characterized by strict adherence to regulations, processes, and close supervision. Moreover, because these organizations are highly dependent on governmental funding, the executive tends to adopt behavior that conforms to standards, policies, criteria, and service programs dictated by the governmental funding agencies (Schmid, 2001). This conformist behavior ensures the institution of stability and a steady flow of resources.

Figure 1. Types of Leadership and Patterns of Management

Task Oriented

I. Task Oriented—Internal

Emphasis on achieving organizational goals, taking the organizational structure and internal work procedures into account.

Emphasis on the roles of planning, coordination, administrative communication, budgeting, and decision making.

Leadership style is authoritative, centralized; no delegation of authority and no involvement of organization members in decision making.

Tight control and supervision, closely linked to processes and outcomes.

The leader does not tolerate deviations from the rules and processes that regulate the life of the organization. Very low tolerance for ambiguity.

III. Task Oriented—External

Leader's behavior focuses on achieving organizational goals and attaining legitimation and resources from the external environment.

Leadership style is authoritative, centralized, directive, and focused on attaining resources, establishing and expanding the organizational domain, improving the organization's competitive ability in an attempt to accumulate an organizational and personal power advantage over other organizations.

Leader is task oriented, without considering the human factor. The human factor is a means to achieve his goals.

Decision-making and problem-solving processes are based on the leader's formal authority.

Internal Orientation ← → *External Orientation*

II. People Oriented—Internal

The leader's main focus is on people. He or she motivates, provides incentives, delegates authority, empowers, consults, and involves others.

Efforts focused on selecting, developing, building, and guiding the staff and co-opting them to achieve the goals of the organization.

Emphasis on division of labor and roles, including enlargement and enrichment.

The leader motivates workers to seek self-fulfillment, sets challenging goals, and encourages self-development.

The leader develops tools, mechanisms, methods, and technologies for problem solving and conflict resolution.

IV. People Oriented—External

Emphasis on managing the external environment, reducing the organization's dependence on agents in the environment, and increasing the dependence of others on the organization.

Considerable investment in developing human resources, training, and preparing staff to cope with constraints imposed on the organization by the external environment.

The leader and administrative staff engage in political activity and form alliances and coalitions with various elements in the environment. Emphasis on alleviating pressure from interest groups and constituencies; screening the environment to identify opportunities, risks, and threats.

Emphasis on the importance and contribution of the human factor; invests in developing the functional maturity and professional competence of the staff in order to allow for development of relations with the external environment and management by exception.

People Oriented

The style of leadership described in quadrant III can also be appropriate in this type of organization. In recent years, residential institutions have encountered increasing competition with private for-profit organizations in the arena of social service provision, which in the past was dominated almost exclusively by nonprofit organizations. Inevitably, these resources, primarily controlled by the government and partially by foundations and private donors, are no longer ensured to nonprofit residential institutions. Consequently, the leaders of those institutions need to channel their efforts toward dealing with the external environment in an attempt to minimize the organization's dependence on external funding agents and rely more on their own professional, organizational, and structural resources. Nonetheless, because of the unique organizational culture of residential institutions, authoritative and centralized management is still the most prevalent. This pattern ensures the organization of the continued stability it needs to serve special and at-risk populations. Professional and administrative staff members usually follow the directions set by the leader, because they recognize that strict adherence to the rules and regulations is essential for maintaining the quality of life among residents of the boarding institutions.

Failure to make the necessary transition from centralized authority to decentralization of powers and authority may prevent the organization from achieving efficiency and organizational effectiveness.

The most appropriate leadership pattern in community service organizations, to my understanding, is described in quadrants II and IV. In the initial stages of the organizational life cycle, the pattern described in quadrant II is most suitable. Afterward, once the organization has become established, the leader should focus on developing the internal organizational system and stabilizing the organization's activities, as well as on building and developing the administrative and professional team. In the early stages of the organization's development, there are no clear patterns of activity, and the founding leader runs a one-person show, where his or her directives obligate the members of the organization. However, at subsequent stages, the leader relies on knowledge and information possessed by staff members in the process of making decisions. At that point, the community service organization needs a division of labor based on delegation of tasks and use of the relative advantages of team members who specialize in various fields and areas. Hence, leaders who fail to understand the changing situation may face the phenomenon of founder's trap: failure to make the necessary transition from centralized authority to decentralization of powers and authority may prevent the organization from achieving efficiency and organizational effectiveness.

At later stages in the development of the community service organization, a change in leadership style can be expected. Undoubtedly the leader has to stabilize the organization's structure from the inside and needs to focus on positioning the organization and ensuring a steady flow of resources in a dynamic, turbulent political environment. Whereas in the past these resources were ensured to community organizations by the government, today the flow of resources from the government is minimal. The organization's revenue derives mainly from sale of services and programs, and some funds are raised from foundations and donors. In the light of the decline in governmental resources and the increasing competition with private for-profit organizations, the most appropriate pattern of leadership at the later stages of development is the one described in quadrant IV. Notably, this style is represented in the transformational leader, who can function best under these conditions because he or she has the vision, determination, and ability to arouse intellectual stimulation and mobilize support among followers. The transformational leader recognizes the need to gain a better understanding of the environment and its political dynamics in the light of stiff competition for scarce resources. Hence, his or her efforts are directed to reducing the organization's dependence on external elements that try to undermine its status. In this context, it is important to manage the environment and map its strengths and weaknesses, opportunities and risks. In community service organizations, this orientation is more important than a strategy that focuses on maintaining existing processes and on routine management of the organization. The external orientation and efforts to scan the environment entail cooperation with other agencies, institutions, and organizations, as well as forming alliances and partnerships with them. Furthermore, leaders in these organizations need to have the vision and political acumen to mobilize support from their staff and ensure the smooth functioning of their organization. Staff members have the potential to assume leadership positions, and their level of professional maturity is relatively high. They are selected for their positions in accordance with criteria such as a high level of formal education, high motivation, ability, and willingness to take on jobs and responsibilities. In these contexts, the appropriate style of leadership is delegation of authority and powers and collaboration (Hersey and Blanchard, 1982). An authoritative, directive style can inhibit initiative, independent thought, and willingness to perform tasks and take responsibility. By developing the staff, delegating authority, and empowering workers, the leader can be free to deal with special issues that arise, while workers with appropriate abilities and functional maturity can take charge of routine tasks and ensure the organization's effective functioning.

Leaders of [home care] organizations need to scan their environment and search for new opportunities.

In the case of home care organizations that provide services to the elderly, the most appropriate leadership style, in my view, is the one presented in quadrant III of Figure 1, which reflects task-oriented behavior and emphasizes relations with the external environment. Whereas the milieu of home care services was dominated by nonprofit organizations in the past, today the share of the private for-profit sector has increased to 70 percent, and the share of the nonprofit sector has diminished to 30 percent. In this situation, it is clear that leaders need to channel their efforts to the external environment, with emphasis on governmental agencies, which provide most of the funding for the organization's activities and service programs. Moreover, in the light of the diminishing share of nonprofit organizations in the market of home care services, nonprofit providers have had to seek other service domains and target populations in order to ensure the flow of income they need for their survival. Toward that end, the leaders of those organizations need to scan their environment and search for new opportunities, while removing existing and potential threats to the organization's stability. At the same time, the pattern of leadership needs to be task oriented, particularly because the staff members are home care workers with a low level of formal education and a low to average level of functional maturity. They receive a limited amount of training, their wages are low, and opportunities for advancement are minimal. The large staff of home care workers is supervised by a small team of professionals such as social workers. Under these circumstances, Hersey and Blanchard (1982) argue, the most appropriate style of leadership is authoritative and task oriented, with very little staff participation. The workers use relatively simple technologies, and the tasks are specified in the care plan dictated by the institution that funds most of the organization's activities.

Finally, in the case of organizations that provide services for children and youth at risk, most of the workers are professionals and volunteer staff, and almost all of the characteristics described in every quadrant of Figure 1 are appropriate. Many organizations that serve children and youth at risk were established by private entrepreneurs who were committed to found an organization that responds to the needs of those children. Therefore, in the initial stages of the organization's development, the founder acts as an entrepreneur, and the main mission is to create a niche in which the organization defines its domain and positions itself. At this stage, the organization is characterized by a high level of informality and lacks clear mechanisms for decision making, coordination, and communication with other members. The external environment is characterized by a high level of uncertainty, because the founding leader lacks sufficient information about the institutions and agencies operating there. Under these conditions, the leader-founder is usually committed to his or her vision and ideals while maintaining a strong task orientation. The leader relies extensively on charisma and concentrates most of the power in his or her own hands without delegating authority or enabling staff members to participate in decision making.

Once the leader-founder succeeds in stabilizing the organization's environment and achieving a steady increase in the number of administrative and professional staff members, the style of leadership will have to be adapted. In my view, the most appropriate style at that point is the one described in quadrant II of Figure 1, which combines people-oriented and internal-oriented leadership because the environment is more certain and the founding leader is more familiar with the agencies operating in it. As the leader tries to position the organization in its domain, he or she also begins to build a team, delegate more authority, and establish a division of labor among the staff members. From the people-oriented perspective, the leader devotes a considerable amount of time to building and developing his or her team while fostering an esprit de corps needed to gain support from the team members. This style of leadership resembles a democratic and participatory one, where team members are encouraged to assume more responsibility. Nonetheless, based on the characteristics of these organizations as described earlier and in the light of the growing competition with for-profit organizations, it appears that the organization requires a new type of leadership—and the most appropriate pattern, in my view, is the one presented in quadrant IV of Figure 1.

Under these circumstances, the leader's orientation should be toward managing the task environment and acquiring more resources, while also delegating authority and power to competent and highly committed followers. The leader needs to develop special skills, particularly in the areas of politics and external relations, in addition to a profound awareness of the changing turbulent environments. At the same time, the leader can adopt people-oriented behavior, because the staff members are professionals whose level of psychological and functional maturity enables them to assume more responsibility. Thus, the leaders can delegate authority and involve their staff in processes of decision making and mobilizing resources. In so doing, they give their workers information and knowledge about the tasks and missions to be performed and strategies for carrying them out, while fostering an esprit de corps and a high level of commitment (Bass and Avolio, 1990).

Conclusion

This article dealt with leadership patterns and their relationships to different types of organizations at various stages of the organizational life cycle. The underlying assumption was that these patterns should vary in accordance with the changing situation and contingencies of the organization. If there is a mismatch between the pattern of leadership and the unique circumstances of the organization, obstacles will be encountered in the attempt to achieve the organization's espoused goals. At the same time, the leader has the power and capacity to have an impact on the organization in accordance with his or her vision, values, codes of behavior, and modes of leadership. In addition, the leader has the ability to inspire the organization, but must be particularly sensitive to its unique culture if he or she wishes to continue leading it.

The basic assumption here is that the ideal situation is one in which the leader is able to adapt his or her behavior in the transition from one stage of the organization's life cycle to another, consistent with the four quadrants presented in Figure 1. This does not always happen, since leaders with specific characteristics and skills can be suitable for one type of organization in a given situation, whereas the same characteristics might not be appropriate at other stages of the organization's development and in other situations or environments. If the leader is unable to adapt his or her behavior patterns to the situation at hand, it is best to choose a new leader with the appropriate qualities. Therefore, the model proposed can be useful for

If the leader is unable to adapt his or her behavior patterns to the situation at hand, it is best to choose a new leader with the appropriate qualities.

boards of directors in the processes of selecting and hiring leaders for their organization. These processes should reflect the changes that take place in the organizational environment, the organization itself, and the organization's human resources.

I am not taking a stand on the issue of whether personality traits or situations make the leader. Rather, I am suggesting a need to integrate all of those elements. The traits and qualities of leaders undoubtedly play an important role in shaping and building the organization and in influencing its culture. Nonetheless, those very characteristics can lead to failure if the organization's specific situation is not properly assessed and the leaders are unable to understand the organization's nature and spirit. Fiedler (1996) argued that "all of the reviews of leadership training . . . stress that we know very little about the processes of leadership and managerial training that contribute to organizational performance" (p. 244). In addition, many researchers have found that it is difficult for people to change their cognitive style of orientation, dominant motives, or global behavior patterns (Fiedler, 1967). However, I propose a different approach: individuals have to make adaptations in their leadership pattern— whether they are autocratic, democratic-participatory, charismatic, task-oriented, or person-oriented—if they wish to be effective and achieve their goals. In the case of organizational leadership, innate characteristics can be affected by the environments in which individuals, groups, and organizations operate, as well as by values, expectations, and behavior of others, and by cultures in general and organizational culture in particular.

I am not claiming that the basic characteristics and style of different leaders can change appreciably. Nonetheless, it is important to develop potential leaders' awareness of different patterns that can be adopted, as well as the ability to recognize their personal strengths and weaknesses. This is particularly true of nonprofit human service and community service organizations, which have to cope with constant transitions and changes, especially in the light of the declining legitimacy of the welfare state. Concomitantly, these organizations have witnessed processes of decentralization, devolution, and outsourcing or contracting out of services. All of these processes require leadership that promotes vision and ideals and is characterized by perseverance, consistency, flexibility, and an orientation toward achieving the organization's goals.

HILLEL SCHMID is professor and dean of the Paul Baerwald School of Social Work and Social Welfare at the Hebrew University of Jerusalem, Israel.

References

Aldrich, H., and Pfeffer, J. "Environments of Organizations." *Annual Review of Sociology,* 1976, *11,* 79–105.

Bargal, D. "The Manager as Leader." In R. Patti (ed.), *The Handbook of Social Welfare Management*. Thousand Oaks, Calif.: Sage, 2001.

Bargal, D., and Guterman, N. "Perceptions of Job Satisfaction, Service Effectiveness and Burnout Among Social Workers in Israel." *Hevra Urevaha [Society and Welfare]*, 1996, *16*, 541–565. (in Hebrew)

Bass, B. M. *Leadership and Performance Beyond Expectations*. New York: Free Press, 1985.

Bass, B. M., and Avolio, B. J. "The Implication of Transactional and Transformational Leadership for Individual, Team, and Organizational Development." *Research in Organizational Change and Development*, 1990, *4*, 231–272.

Bennis, W., and Nanus, B. *Leaders: The Strategies for Taking Charge*. New York: HarperCollins, 1985.

Burns, J. M. *Leadership*. New York: HarperCollins, 1978.

Conger, J. A., and Kanungo, R. A. "Toward a Behavioral Theory of Charismatic Leadership in Organizational Settings." *Academy of Management Review*, 1987, *12*, 637–647.

Dvir, T., Eden, D., Avolio, B. J., and Shamir, B. "Impact of Transformational Leadership on Follower Development and Performance: A Field Experiment." *Academy of Management Journal*, 2002, *45*, 735–744.

Fiedler, F. E. *A Theory of Leadership Effectiveness*. New York: McGraw-Hill, 1967.

Fiedler, F. E. "A Rejoinder to Schriesheim and Kerr's Premature Obituary of the Contingency Model." In J. G. Hunt and L. L. Larson (eds.), *Leadership: The Cutting Edge*. Carbondale: Southern Illinois University Press, 1977.

Fiedler, F. E. "Research on Leadership Selection and Training: One View of the Future." *Administrative Science Quarterly*, 1996, *41*, 241–250.

Fiedler, F. E., and Garcia, J. E. *New Approaches to Effective Leadership: Cognitive Resources and Organizational Performance*. Hoboken, N.J.: Wiley, 1987.

Halpin, A. W. *The Leadership Behavior of School Superintendents*. Chicago: Midwest Administration Center, University of Chicago, 1959.

Hemphill, J. V. *Situational Factors in Leadership*. Columbus, Ohio: Bureau of Educational Research, Ohio State University, 1949.

Hersey, P., and Blanchard, K. *Management of Organizational Behavior: Utilizing Human Resources*. Upper Saddle River, N.J.: Prentice Hall, 1982.

House, R. J. "A Path Goal Theory of Leader Effectiveness." *Administrative Science Quarterly*, 1971, *16*, 321–338.

House, R. J. "A 1976 Theory of Charismatic Leadership." In J. G. Hunt and L. L. Larson (eds.), *Leadership: The Cutting Edge*. Carbondale: Southern Illinois University Press, 1977.

House, R. J., and Aditya, R. N. "The Social Scientific Study of Leaders: Qua Vadis?" *Journal of Management*, 1997, *23* (3), 409–473.

House, R. J., and Baetz, M. "Leadership: Some Empirical Generalization and New Research Directions." In B. Staw (ed.), *Research in Organizational Behavior* (Vol. 1). Greenwich, Conn.: JAI Press, 1979.

House, R. J., and Mitchell, T. R. "Path-Goal Theory of Leadership." *Journal of Contemporary Business,* 1974, 3, 81–97.

House, R. J., Shane, S., and Herold, D. "Rumors of the Death of Dispositional Theory and Research in Organizational Behavior Are Greatly Exaggerated." *Academy of Management Review,* 1996, 21, 203–204.

Kendall, J., and Knapp, M. "A Loose and Baggy Monster: Boundaries and Definitions in the Voluntary Sector." In J. Davis-Smith, C. Rochester, and R. Heley (eds.), *Introduction to the Voluntary Sector.* London: Routledge, 1995.

Likert, R. *New Patterns of Management.* New York: McGraw-Hill, 1961.

Mirvis, R. "The Quality of Employment in the Nonprofit Sector: An Update of Employee Attitudes in Nonprofit versus Business and Government." *Nonprofit Management and Leadership,* 1992, 3, 23–42.

Nanus, B. *Visionary Leadership: Creating a Compelling Sense of Direction for Your Organization.* San Francisco: Jossey-Bass, 1992.

Schmid, H. "Relationships Between Decentralized Authority and Other Structural Properties in Human Service Organizations: Implications for Service Effectiveness." *Administration in Social Work,* 1992a, 16, 25–39.

Schmid, H. "Executive Leadership in Human Service Organizations." In Y. Hasenfeld (ed.), *Human Services as Complex Organizations.* Thousand Oaks, Calif.: Sage, 1992b.

Schmid, H. "Evaluating the Impact of Legal Change on Nonprofit and For-Profit Organizations: The Case of the Israeli Long-Term Care Insurance Law." *Public Management Review,* 2001, 3 (2), 167–189.

Schmid, H., and Bar-Nir, D. "The Relationship Between Organizational Properties and Service Effectiveness in Residential Boarding Schools." *Children and Youth Services Review,* 2001, 23, 243–271.

Schmid, H., and Nirel, R. "Relationships Between Organizational Properties and Service Effectiveness in Home Care Organizations." *Journal of Social Service Research,* 1995, 20 (3/4), 71–92.

Schmid, H., and others. *Voluntary Nonprofit Human Service Organizations Delivering Services to Children and Adolescents: Areas of Activity and Structure.* Jerusalem: Graduate Program in the Management of Voluntary Nonprofit Organizations, Hebrew University of Jerusalem, 2001. (in Hebrew)

Stogdill, R. M., and Coons, A. E. *Leader Behavior: Its Description and Measurement.* Columbus, Ohio: State University Press for Bureau of Business Research, 1957.

Vroom, V. H., and Yetton, P. W. *Leadership and Decision Making.* Pittsburgh: University of Pittsburgh Press, 1973.

For bulk reprints of this article, please call (201) 748-8789.

How Does Accountability Affect Mission?

The Case of a Nonprofit Serving Immigrants and Refugees

Rachel A. Christensen,
Alnoor Ebrahim

This article examines accountability processes in a nonprofit organization serving immigrants and refugees, with special attention to their impacts on mission-based activities. The research finds that upward accountability requirements of donors do not necessarily yield improved mission achievement, and practitioners thus have to navigate a complex environment of pressures. We identify a series of strategies that nonprofit executives and staff use to manage the tensions between upward accountability and mission: a prioritization of lateral accountability, staff empowerment through organizational slack, and a tight coupling of evaluation with job tasks. The findings suggest that funders and nonprofits might gain more from investing in internal grantee capacities for lateral communication and coordination than by soliciting more detailed reporting.

NONPROFITS HAVE HISTORICALLY operated in a sector that some have considered above criticism. Times are changing, however, and nonprofit status no longer places an organization beyond reproach. Today, nonprofit organizations are expected to incorporate multiple systems of accountability that identify outcomes and demonstrate transparency in financing and decision making. Accordingly, scholars have noted a growing attention in the sector toward increased reporting, auditing, and monitoring activities (Edwards and Hulme, 1996b; Kearns, 1996; Najam, 1996). These mechanisms are generally put into place to provide accountability to funders, donors, and oversight agencies. Two fundamental questions remain: Does this added attention to upward accountability enhance organizational mission, and how do practitioners maintain their focus on mission in the face of stringent reporting demands? The research literature suggests that upward

NONPROFIT MANAGEMENT & LEADERSHIP, vol. 17, no. 2, Winter 2006   © 2006 Wiley Periodicals, Inc.   **195**
Published online in Wiley InterScience (www.interscience.wiley.com). DOI: 10.1002/nml.143

accountability demands may be too intense for many nonprofit organizations and may threaten downward and lateral accountability or even the mission of the organization.

A key purpose of this article is to examine how these accountability pressures play out in day-to-day organizational life, and thus to shed light on their impacts on managerial practice and mission. More specifically, we explore the relationships between accountability mechanisms and mission-based activities in a nonprofit organization serving immigrants and refugees. Nonprofit and public organizations currently provide services to nearly 30 million immigrants and refugees in the United States. For the purposes of this research, a mechanism is defined as a process or technique employed for achieving a result. Accountability mechanisms are distinct activities or processes designed to ensure particular kinds of results.

Nonprofit Accountability

Nonprofit organizations are expected to incorporate multiple systems of accountability that identify outcomes and demonstrate transparency in financing and decision making.

Accountability is "generally interpreted as the means by which individuals and organizations report to a recognized authority . . . and are held responsible for their actions" (Edwards and Hulme, 1996b, p. 8). Default descriptions of nonprofit accountability environments tend to emphasize answerability to donors, funding sources, and government and ensuring that money is spent consistently with the donor's wishes (Najam, 1996). In addition, during the past decade, "government regulation and oversight of nonprofit service organizations have grown substantially" (Smith and Lipsky, 1993, p. 79), attempting to ensure nonprofit organization accountability to the public. These accountability requirements are part of a larger trend across the service provision sector, affecting both public agencies and private providers. In other words, accountability in public service contracting has focused on principal-agent relationships of rules, after-the-fact answerability, and punishment.

Other views of accountability have broadened the discussion, focusing on both being held responsible by others and taking responsibility for oneself (Fry, 1995). In this view, accountability is "not only a reactive response to overseers, but also a proactive one linked to ensuring that the public trust is served" (Ebrahim, 2003, p. 194). According to this broader definition, used in this article, accountability refers to being answerable to stakeholders for the actions of the organization, whether by internal or external initiation. Thus, nonprofit organizations can be accountable on multiple levels: upward, lateral, and downward, at the very least.

Upward accountability usually is conceptualized as being held accountable from above. Lateral and downward accountability are more often a result of felt responsibility; both use less formalized methods, so it is not always clear how agencies can realize accountability on these levels. Najam (1996, p. 352) states that nongovernmental organizations (NGOs) must "begin creating mechanisms and organizational structures that are equally account-able to their patrons, their clients, and to their own selves." These mechanisms are likely to vary by organization type: those in service delivery organizations (such as refugee resettlement agencies) will be different from those in grassroots membership organizations (such as cooperatives or self-help groups), for example. The latter type of organization is more structurally amenable to downward accountability, particularly when its members are its clients and members engage in participatory decision making (Smith, 1999, p. 105). In a cooperative, for example, the mechanisms of account-ability available to members include franchise (voting for the orga-nization's leaders), revoking membership and dues (and joining another cooperative, for instance), limiting terms of office and peri-odic job rotation for those in authority positions, and attempting to reform the organization either by influencing leaders or by running for a leadership position (Rothschild and Whitt, 1986).

Presumably, if lateral and downward forms of accountability are important to nonprofit agencies, they must develop methods to scru-tinize and build accountability to lateral and downward stakeholders. However, many practitioners and scholars have expressed concerns regarding the "difficulties [nonprofit organizations] face in prioritiz-ing and reconciling these multiple accountabilities" (Edwards and Hulme, 1996a, p. 968), especially in cases where accountability is "skewed to the most powerful constituency." The case study reported here demonstrates how these multiple accountabilities play out in day-to-day organizational life and the strategies organizational staff use to cope and prioritize their accountabilities while striving to meet the organization's mission.

If lateral and downward forms of accountability are important to nonprofit agencies, they must develop methods to scrutinize and build accountability to lateral and downward stakeholders.

The Case and Research Methods

Ten private national voluntary agencies are central to the U.S. refugee resettlement program, providing coordinated services supported through both private and government funding (U.S. Department of Health and Human Services, 2002). Nine of these organizations are religiously affiliated, and they work with more than 450 local reset-tlement offices throughout the country to assist refugees in adjust-ing to their new homes, surroundings, and cities.

This study focuses on Bright Star (a pseudonym for confiden-tiality reasons), a local refugee resettlement and immigration assis-tance agency that is part of one of the nine religiously affiliated national voluntary organizations working with the U.S. Department of State. Bright Star, which has fourteen full-time staff members and a community board of twelve members, has served its region for over twenty-five years and resettles approximately two hundred refugees each year. In addition, it connects refugees to sources of social services and national assistance.

Bright Star is fairly representative of refugee resettlement agencies in that it receives federal funding through the U.S. Department of State as well as a balance of national voluntary agency and foundation funding. Accordingly, it engages in multiple upward accountability activities related to these funding and regulatory streams.

Fieldwork for this research was conducted between January 2001 and March 2002 by the first author of this article. Data collection included field observations, interviews, and document analysis (Merriam, 1998). Accountability demands and relationships at Bright Star were explored using an interpretive approach (Neuman, 2003) with the expectation that the case would uncover a series of propositions and insights of broader analytical and theoretical import (Yin, 2003) concerning how competing accountability demands play out in an organizational context and how nonprofit staff negotiate these tensions in order to meet organizational mission. Two broad propositions and three subpropositions emerging from this case are highlighted in our conclusions.

At Bright Star, upward accountability is achieved through highly personalized efforts to detail how money and resources are used.

The Interplay of Nonprofit Accountabilities and Mission

Not surprisingly, the director and staff of Bright Star see themselves as accountable along three different levels or dimensions: (1) upward to individual donors, funders, and their national voluntary agency; (2) laterally to one another and themselves, as the staff, volunteers, community board members, and the community agencies with whom they work; and (3) downward to their clients and beneficiaries and the local community. Each level of accountability requires different kinds of mechanisms (with some overlap across levels). These mechanisms range from being a formal component of the institutional structure, such as reports, to an informal element of the structure, such as open dialogue among staff. Table 1 summarizes various mechanisms of accountability used by Bright Star.

Upward Accountability: Counting Spoons and Other Tedious Measures

At Bright Star, upward accountability is achieved through highly personalized efforts to detail how money and resources are used. Fundraising letters and thank-you letters to individual donors explain how money is being used. Accountability to funders is achieved through multiple reports on a monthly or quarterly basis as well as audits and monitoring visits. The five most significant reports in terms of funding percentage and paperwork requirements are outlined in Table 2. (The names of some of the reports have been changed for confidentiality reasons.)

According to Bright Star's director, all of this reporting can become "very tedious." This is perhaps best exemplified by the

Table 1. Bright Star's Accountability Mechanisms

	Accountability to Whom?	*Accountability Mechanisms*
Upward accountability	• Donors • Funders • National voluntary agency	• Reports to the national voluntary agency • Audits • Case notes in client files • Caseworker time and mileage form • Monitoring visits • Reports to funders • Donor thank-you letters • Transparency in fundraising letters to potential donors
Lateral accountability	• Staff and board • Mission • Volunteers • Community partners	• Staff meetings • Informal open communication among staff • Staff performance self-evaluations • Case notes in client files • Director support of staff • Volunteer exit interviews • Volunteer tutor training • Monthly peer and volunteer tutor report forms • Telephone conversations and messages with peer and volunteer tutors • Alignment of fee-for-service component to agency mission • Cultural training for other agencies • Access to ESL resources • Focus groups to prepare agencies for large arrivals • Attending school board meetings • Regular contact with schools • Participation in community associations
Downward accountability	• Clients and beneficiaries	• Voice mail in clients' native languages • Needs assessments • Documents, pamphlets, and brochures in native languages • Access to caseworkers and the director of agency • Client evaluation of English tutoring program • Weekly caseworker and staff visits to clients' homes • Organizational slack that allows prioritization of client needs • Agreement in the client's native language outlining services • Cultural training for other agencies • Focus groups with experts to prepare for new arrivals • Transparency with news media • Regular contact with schools

matching grant report, which is designed to ensure matching for all donations. The director describes it as "a tedious report, as it is the accumulation of all knowledge about a client or family." It is the most intensive of all the reports, requiring detailed accounting of the time and activities of caseworkers, time and mileage of tutors, donations of

Table 2. Major Funding Sources and Upward Accountability Reports Overview

Report	Purpose of Funds	Source of Funds	Type of Report	Monthly/ Quarterly	Activities to Complete Report	Purpose of Report
National voluntary agency	Provide initial resettlement assistance	Federal, state	Programmatic: Narrative and statistical	Monthly and quarterly	Talk with all caseworkers; gather documentation on each case/family	Overview of the services provided
Matching grant	Provide alternative to public assistance	Federal	Fiscal	Monthly	Home visits to count items; review tutor reports	Document the number of items and services donated
Support for families	Strengthen families, focusing on English education and the school-parent-child tie	Federal	Programmatic: Narrative and numerical	Quarterly	Review personnel notes and charts; director compiles organizationwide report and assembles statistics and narratives from multiple components of agency; review information on each client regarding education services provided	Overview of the services provided to support refugee families
Mental health	Assist with refugee adjustment to life in the United States	Federal	Programmatic	Quarterly	Staff meetings and informal discussions with staff to gather information	Overview of services provided
State report	Provide statewide services to refugees through contracts with voluntary agencies	Federal, through the state	Programmatic: Numerical with narrative components	Quarterly	Review all case files; enter all services provided to each case/family; use numerical report to inform a narrative	Track the services statewide; police contracts for federal funding

items and food, and employment searches. The volunteer coordinator completes four different forms each month and must visit client homes and count items, sometimes having to "dig through cabinets and drawers to determine the number of extra items like towels, blankets" that exceed a family's immediate needs "in excess of the number of people in the home." The report is "very detailed, and [it] takes forever to count each item and assess its value. I can only count that which is [deemed] extra, what is beyond what they need . . . for example, the number of chairs, you can count chairs in excess of the number of people in the home." This report, which requires a literal counting of the number of spoons donated to families, is meant to demonstrate that Bright Star has accounted for everything given to a client.

The image of a practitioner digging through drawers and counting spoons raises several questions about the upward accountability requirements faced by Bright Star. Is spoon counting the best use of a practitioner's time? Does it lead to better service provision? Does knowing the number of spoons given to a client help the funding agency know how clients are being served and whether the organization's mission is being achieved?

There are at least two major unintended effects of a focus on "spoon counting." First, practitioners begin to absorb the subtle messages sent by such reporting requirements and thus can focus on activities that are the easiest to implement and measure rather than considering the best course of action for meeting the organization's mission. In this case, the question sometimes becomes, "How many spoons can I give this client?" rather than, "What does this client need in order to be resettled?" Indeed, Bright Star staff members are concerned about the impacts of reporting demands on the organization's capacity to meet its mission. The director of Bright Star acknowledges that "the reporting requirements serve a purpose," but she believes that "the people who write the requirements don't have a clue what the organization does. They need to look beyond [counting] spoons to [valuing] the intangibles. . . . There is no way to account for so many things that we do." And requirements tend to be duplicative, with "six or seven federal grants, all requiring different reports. . . . If the federal government could consolidate and say this is what we expect, you could get it down to two reports."

Bright Star's director has set up a number of buffers to protect staff from these demands. She tries to "make it as simple as possible for the staff" by keeping "grant paper-pushing" in perspective and secondary to organizational mission. Along those lines, she has negotiated with auditors to make certain forms as usable as possible for staff members. By taking an active role in determining what is reported, she tries to minimize paperwork while working to ensure that the information is useful to the organization. For example, she worked with federal and state auditors to combine the record of

By taking an active role in determining what is reported, [the director] tries to minimize paperwork while working to ensure that the information is useful to the organization.

time spent with families and mileage sheets because "it would be impossible to note the time spent with individual families, as a caseworker could be dealing with multiple cases at once and . . . would end up spending all of their time writing in time sheets."

A second major effect of spoon counting has been the monopolization of time that could otherwise be spent in ways more useful to the organization. Some reports generated for funders do not necessarily help Bright Star further its mission. Staff members readily admit that they see little use in reports that are simple compilations of what they do monthly. The purpose of such reports was succinctly stated by Bright Star's education coordinator: "This [report] does not add anything, except that it sustains our program, as it gives money for our staff. . . . It is not that useful. It inhibits us. I don't see much value in it. It is a numbers game. I know we need to do it for funders."

This does not mean, however, that staff members are unwilling to engage in time-consuming reporting. On the contrary, staff are at times quite willing to engage in cumbersome and demanding reporting when it is aligned with their sense of organizational purpose. For example, many staff members perceive the matching grant report (which includes spoon counting) as useful and valuable to Bright Star. Although the report requires detailed accounting, home visits, and review of forms, and takes considerable time, it is seen as important because "it keeps us organized, keeps us up-to-date on what donations our families are getting, services, tutor time. Not all families are [a part of this program], but it is nice to have a representative show of our families." The key point is that the feelings of the staff toward upward accountability activities are directly related to how useful they perceive reports to be. Actual time commitments are less important than whether staff members can directly identify how reporting is connected to the mission-based activities of their organization. Unfortunately, the majority of reports were seen as disconnected from mission and created a variety of tensions for practitioners who wanted to be serving clients but instead found themselves gathering data and compiling reports that served only the purpose of keeping the funding flowing.

Organizational Strategies for Managing Tensions

Given the demands of upward reporting, a number of understudied questions remain. How do organizations manage the tensions brought about by overly detailed and unrelated reporting and auditing requirements? When accountability to funders does not ensure accountability to other organizational stakeholders, how can practitioners maintain accountability to one another, partner agencies, and clients? How can nonprofit staff operating within the demands of contracting relationships maintain a focus on mission?

The case of Bright Star points to three mediating factors for managing these tensions: a prioritization of lateral accountability, staff empowerment through organizational slack, and a tight coupling of evaluation with job tasks.

Prioritizing Lateral Accountability: Focusing on Staff. Navigating the variety of demands in nonprofit service provision is difficult work. It thus begs the question of how nonprofit organizations can help support staff members in reconciling multiple accountabilities and staying focused on mission. The director of Bright Star answers this question by explaining her "personal philosophy . . . that staff are the first priority and the second priority is the people they serve." She always "back[s] [staff] up and trust[s] them. Then, they can do their job with total focus without worry." She says that she tries "to be as open to the staff as [she] can be." The director has developed a principle of supporting her staff in a way that she identifies as different from profit-focused management: "You get a different breed of people in this type of work, people who love their work, who are committed to the work, but maybe people whose needs are greater than others. . . . They feel a real need to give, but you have to adjust your management style for that." Through a focus on "her" people so they can focus on "their" people, Bright Star's director sets the stage for lateral and downward accountability to emerge naturally.

Weekly staff meetings provide a forum for accountability to each other as well as ensure better responsiveness to client needs. These meetings are seen as crucial for coordinating services so that, for example, educational tutoring and medical appointments can be coordinated with clients' work schedules. During one staff meeting, each of the staff members spoke about the activities he or she had engaged in during the past week and highlighted any important upcoming events. Then the staff spent more than an hour discussing each of the families, beginning with the most recent arrival. They informed each other of what was happening with each family in relation to donations, needs, doctor appointments, tutor activities, and medical situations, among other things. They discussed all of the contact that each staff member had with that family during the last week. Then as a group, they determined what steps should be taken and by whom for each family. This information was entered into a log recording each week's decisions. Staff members also used this time to inform one another of services that might address concerns regarding different families. These meetings are foundational for staff members to remain answerable to one another for their actions, while also ensuring increased attention to client needs.

Bright Star staff members are highly accessible to one another, with the physical setup of the office space designed to encourage impromptu and informal coordination. By locating her work space in an accessible way, the director promotes informal interactions among staff members. In addition, staff members maintain contact through frequent notes in one another's mailboxes. The case notes in client files allow staff to access information on what is happening

Navigating the variety of demands in nonprofit service provision is difficult work.

with the clients or beneficiaries when other forms of communication are not available.

In short, staff members have frequent informal gatherings to work together on different cases or families. These discussions allow them the opportunity to rely on one another for relevant expertise and overall support. While these practices may seem self-evident to some observers, they are less ad hoc than they might appear. The informality is highly structured through multiple mechanisms: the deliberative nature of weekly staff meetings, the physical setup of office space, and the normative expectation that all staff are to stay informed of the status of clients, including those with whom they do not directly work. The director plays a pivotal coordinating function that enables staff to discuss their experiences in relation to one another, their clients or beneficiaries, and the agencies with which they work. Enabling interaction is part of a deliberate strategy to create open communication among staff members, with the explicit purpose of improving accountability and ensuring better service provision. The supportive infrastructure of the organization's culture is purposeful. Lateral accountability among staff thus ensures better downward accountability by making clients a focal point rather than the rules and checklists often provided by funders.

Staff Empowerment Through Organizational Slack. Bright Star staff members recognize the importance of rules in determining a course of action, but feel supported in making decisions that will best serve their clients and meet the organization's mission rather than ensure that it is "audit proof." The organization builds in slack to allow for flexibility and innovation (Scott, 2003). By empowering staff to act and not demanding an accounting of every action, organizational "slack . . . provides some ease in the system" and thus enables a focus on mission achievement beyond regulations (Scott, 2003, p. 237).

Although compliance with upward accountability mechanisms is a high priority in Bright Star, staff members have sometimes deliberately engaged in activities that are not among the approved activities of the organization—with the explicit purpose of improving services to clients. In doing so, they clearly prioritize accountability to their clients over all other accountabilities. For example, the caseworkers adopted an informal "don't tell" policy for the benefit of their clients. One caseworker explained that a refugee found out she was pregnant shortly after arriving from a refugee camp. Although the organization would not endorse a visit to a family planning clinic to explore the client's options, the caseworker assisted the refugee in making an appointment at the client's request. What mattered to the caseworker was providing information and services to meet refugee needs. Another caseworker clarified this point, noting that if something needed to be done for a client that was not in the caseworker job description or was against the religious values of the national voluntary agency affiliation, the caseworker would "use my own

> *Lateral accountability among staff ensures better downward accountability by making clients a focal point.*

time. . . . On my own time, I can do what I want." Organizational slack enabled the caseworker to remain true to a personal sense of responsibility without compromising organizational accountability.

Tight Coupling of Evaluation with Job Tasks. Bright Star staff members often view lateral and downward accountability activities as simply part of doing their jobs. Downward accountability, including needs assessments and evaluations, is seen by the staff as fundamental to serving clients. Rather than thinking of their activities in terms of accountability, staff members connect these actions to doing their jobs well. Accordingly, they view activities such as needs assessments and evaluations as necessary to know that they are meeting client needs rather than as formal mechanisms for ensuring accountability downward.

Bright Star takes client opinions into consideration when making decisions about organizational priorities and actions. Refugees are asked to complete needs assessment surveys regarding programs. Recently, Bright Star administered a mental health survey asking if refugees would be interested in mental health programs and, if so, what type. The responses led to a grant focused on mental health, allowing Bright Star to provide counseling to clients to assist them in adjusting to life in the United States. The education coordinator notes that the agency has implemented a new program "of asking refugees how they feel about their English program, allowing them to evaluate the program . . . to understand how we can better meet their language needs." She hopes to use this survey to improve the English-language tutoring program by focusing more directly on the needs clients identify.

Bright Star also hosts focus groups of previous arrivals to prepare for the arrival of new populations. According to the agency's director, these discussions center on how needs were met and what the organization could have done differently to welcome the refugee to the region. Staff members frequently engage in needs assessments and evaluations not because of funder requirements but because they seek information regarding the fit of their services with client needs.

In addition to needs assessments, all refugees have multiple meetings with their caseworker during their first three months. This process includes time to talk, ask questions, and give feedback. The initial meetings allow the clients to inform Bright Star through the caseworkers of their needs, as well as ask questions about the services available to them. In these meetings, refugees are provided an agreement form in their native language that outlines what the client can expect from the agency and what he or she must do in terms of working with the agency to meet resettlement needs. The caseworker explains to the beneficiary that she can then use that document to hold the agency accountable for the services it is supposed to provide.

Evaluative practice is effectively coupled with job tasks in Bright Star. However, while client experiences and opinions are included in the organization's decision matrices, accountability mechanisms to clients are decidedly less formal than those to funders. It is thus less clear how clients would hold the organization to account if, in fact, staff members did not view the integration of client voice as important to mission achievement.

Bright Star receives a lot of feedback from clients, volunteers, and partner agencies in both formal and informal ways. Client needs assessments and evaluations were seen as fundamental to the organization because they allow the organization to develop programs that the refugees identify as important. Regular feedback from volunteer tutors provides useful information for making decisions about organizational actions and service provision. Organizational staff stay in touch with partner agencies in a variety of ways, integrating their needs and abilities into decisions about how the organization should approach service provision to clients. Thus, a variety of feedback is used to ensure that quality services are provided, meeting the desires of upward accountability, as well as to ensure that attention is paid to accountability to staff, clients, volunteers, and community partner agencies. The case of Bright Star points to the fact that allowing staff members the space to focus on getting their jobs done may allow lateral and downward accountability to occur more naturally. Simultaneously, multiple accountabilities are served.

Accountability documentation requirements do not always impede the functions and mission-based activities of nonprofit agencies.

Conclusions and Implications

Prior to conducting this research, there was reason to believe that upward accountability demands may be too intense for nonprofit organizations to meet, inhibiting downward and lateral accountability and mission-based activities (Light, 2000; Edwards and Hulme, 1996b; Meyer, 1999). The case of Bright Star points to two main conclusions on the interplay among accountability mechanisms and mission in nonprofit organizations.

First, it is important to note that accountability documentation requirements do not always impede the functions and mission-based activities of nonprofit agencies. In fact, in some cases, they enhance them. Staff do not shy away from highly demanding reporting (which may include counting every spoon donated to a client), but only when they see the relevance of that reporting to their own mission. Similarly, upward reporting that is perceived as lacking utility (regardless of its simplicity) is taken to be onerous and of little value. In other words, if funders and regulators wish nonprofits to internalize their demands for accountability through reporting, it might be worthwhile to consider how those demands can be made more useful to those they are intended to benefit.

Second, an organizational environment that empowers and supports staff members can lead to improved accountability on all levels while better ensuring mission achievement. Such empowerment of collective decision making among staff members allows for felt responsibility, an internal compass, to guide accountability practices of staff. Moreover, it allows staff to focus on doing their jobs well, which includes multiple accountabilities to achieve mission and ensure that funder requirements are met. This leads to three subpropositions.

First, upward and downward accountability can be better achieved with strong lateral accountability mechanisms in place. Activities designed to facilitate lateral accountability, such as staff meetings and community training, have the added benefit of improving other levels of accountability. Bright Star's staff meetings were not only crucial for checking that clients and beneficiaries were receiving the services they had requested, but they also served as a foundation for informal coordination among staff. Staff meetings were also necessary for keeping track of funder requirements. Although these meetings were informal on the surface, they were structured into the organization's operation and thus served as a regular check on client needs. The broader implication of this finding is that attention to improving internal organizational decision processes can improve accountability to all constituents. Therefore, funders and regulators who want better accountability from their grantees might gain more from investing in internal capacity building (especially on communication and coordination issues) among their grantees than by demanding more detailed reporting.

Second, upward accountability stems from being held accountable, while downward and lateral accountability depend more on felt responsibility. There are numerous formalized mechanisms for holding nonprofits upwardly accountable. Many of these mechanisms, such as reporting and disclosure requirements, are contractual or punitive in nature. Mechanisms for downward and lateral accountability are less institutionalized and tend to rely on a felt responsibility by staff. In Bright Star, for example, this felt responsibility pushes staff the extra mile to seek jobs for refugees that include benefits packages rather than simply stopping short at jobs without benefits (which would still satisfy their upward accountability requirements). It is also felt responsibility that pushes staff to go beyond the minimum services required by the rules. A potential disadvantage of relying on felt responsibility for downward accountability is that it places the onus on staff, with little option for recourse by clients. At Bright Star, this problem was partially mitigated by a tight coupling of evaluation with job tasks.

Third, staff often view lateral and downward accountability activities not as accountability mechanisms but as activities that are fundamental to mission-based activity. Activities that provide opportunities for feedback from lateral and downward stakeholders (that is, staff and clients) serve two functions: they broaden the organization's accountabilities while also ensuring better mission achievement. The implication for funders interested in long-term outcomes is that while upward mechanisms are oriented primarily to the measurement of outcomes, downward and lateral mechanisms can enable the achievement of those outcomes (and mission).

A central challenge for nonprofits and funders alike lies in creating a culture of accountability that is built on mission and purpose rather than on external scrutiny. In the words of the philosopher Onora O'Neill: "Perhaps the culture of accountability that we are relentlessly building for ourselves actually damages trust rather than supporting it. Plants don't flourish when we pull them up too often to check how their roots are growing: political, institutional, and professional life may not flourish if we constantly uproot it to demonstrate that everything is transparent and trustworthy" (O'Neill, 2002, p. 19).

The case of Bright Star suggests that the path toward a flourishing and accountable organization may lie within organizational capacities and leadership to mediate the tensions among multiple accountabilities. It is in the very roots of the organization that we find the strength to overcome the often counterproductive pull of upward accountability. Much of what it takes to achieve the mission of Bright Star happens informally, yet informality does not mean ad hoc or unstructured behavior. Creating an organizational culture of trust requires deliberately building the capacity of staff to respond to upward accountability demands while minimizing any negative impact these demands might have on mission achievement.

> *A central challenge for nonprofits and funders alike lies in creating a culture of accountability that is built on mission and purpose rather than on external scrutiny.*

RACHEL A. CHRISTENSEN *is a doctoral candidate in the School of Public and International Affairs at Virginia Polytechnic Institute and State University, focusing on nonprofit organizational governance and accountability.*

ALNOOR EBRAHIM *is a visiting associate professor at the Hauser Center for Nonprofit Organizations at Harvard University and the Wyss visiting scholar at the Harvard Business School. He is the coeditor, with Edward Weisband, of* Forging Global Accountabilities: Participation, Pluralism, and Public Ethics *(forthcoming).*

References

Ebrahim, A. "Making Sense of Accountability: Conceptual Perspectives for Northern and Southern Nonprofits." *Nonprofit Management and Leadership,* 2003, *14* (2), 191–212.

Edwards, M., and Hulme, D. "Too Close for Comfort? The Impact of Official Aid on Nongovernmental Organizations." *World Development,* 1996a, *24* (6), 961–973.

Edwards, M., and Hulme, D. *Beyond the Magic Bullet.* West Bloomfield, Conn.: Kumarian Press, 1996b.

Fry, R. E. "Accountability in Organizational Life: Problem or Opportunity for Nonprofits?" *Nonprofit Management and Leadership,* 1995, *6* (2), 181–195.

Kearns, K. P. *Managing for Accountability: Preserving the Public Trust in Public and Nonprofit Organizations.* San Francisco: Jossey-Bass, 1996.

Light, P. C. *Making Nonprofits Work: A Report on the Tides of Nonprofit Management Reform.* Washington, D.C.: Aspen Institute, Brookings Institution Press, 2000.

Merriam, S. B. *Qualitative Research and Case Study Applications in Education.* San Francisco: Jossey-Bass, 1998.

Meyer, C. A. *The Economics and Politics of NGOs in Latin America.* Westport, Conn.: Praeger, 1999.

Najam, A. "NGO Accountability: A Conceptual Framework." *Development Policy Review,* 1996, *14,* 339–353.

Neuman, W. L. *Social Research Methods: Qualitative and Quantitative Approaches.* (5th ed.) Needham Heights, Mass.: Allyn and Bacon, 2003.

O'Neill, O. *A Question of Trust.* Cambridge: Cambridge University Press, 2002.

Rothschild, J., and Whitt, J. A. *The Cooperative Workplace: Potentials and Dilemmas of Organizational Democracy and Participation.* Cambridge: Cambridge University Press, 1986.

Scott, W. R. *Organizations: Rational, Natural, and Open Systems.* (5th ed.) Upper Saddle River, N.J.: Prentice Hall, 2003.

Smith, D. H. "The Effective Grassroots Association II: Organizational Factors That Produce External Impact." *Nonprofit Management and Leadership,* 1999, *10* (1), 101–116.

Smith, S. R., and Lipsky, M. *Nonprofits for Hire: The Welfare State in the Age of Contracting.* Cambridge, Mass.: Harvard University Press, 1993.

U.S. Department of Health and Human Services. "Overview of the U.S. Resettlement Process." Retrieved Mar. 11, 2002, from http://www.acf.dhhs.gov/programs/orr/programs/overviewrp.htm.

Yin, R. K. *Case Study Research: Design and Methods.* (3rd ed.) Thousand Oaks, Calif.: Sage, 2003.

Interorganizational Trust, Boundary Spanning, and Humanitarian Relief Coordination

Max Stephenson Jr.,
Marcy H. Schnitzer

This article examines the frequently cited argument that coordination issues in humanitarian relief can be addressed more effectively with greater centralized authority and argues for a new conceptualization of aid delivery. The former position suggests a hierarchical, top-down view of the humanitarian relief theater, while this analysis contends that the relief implementation structure may be better conceived as consisting of a network of loosely coupled semiautonomous organizations (Weick, 1976). A network approach allows examination of aid coordination dynamics at multiple levels of analysis: individual (professional and personal), organizational and interorganizational (operational), and strategic (structural/contextual). So viewed, factors that influence relief delivery, including contextual or strategic conditions and organization-scale concerns, may either encourage or dissuade coordination across institutional boundaries. We argue that trust is a key precondition to coordination and that its extension is in turn conditioned by a number of strategic and operating-level factors. We concentrate on operational coordination, as strategic concerns are not often open to the control of lone organizational actors. Our analysis rests in part on in-depth interviews (each consisted of open-ended questions and lasted an average of ninety to one hundred minutes) with a small sample of experienced international nongovernmental organization relief professionals who were engaged in aid efforts in Kosovo following the 1999 intervention by the North Atlantic Treaty Organization in that region.

Note: We thank Kate Lanham and Nicole Kehler for their research in support of this article.

H UMANITARIAN RELIEF ORGANIZATION COORDINATION has been widely researched in recent years (for example, Minear, 2002; Macrae and Harmer, 2003; Rey, 1999). Scholars, as well as aid professionals, funders, and United Nations representatives, have recognized harmonization as a pressing issue. All agree that more successful interorganizational cooperation will yield improved outcomes for those being served. However, factors both internal and external to aid delivery add to the complexities and challenges that attend attainment of successful coordination (Van de Ven and Walker, 1984).

Studies of humanitarian aid delivery have routinely concluded that these complex crises provide an inhospitable setting for coordination (Minear, 2002; Stockton, 2002; Stephenson, 2005, 2006). There are many reasons that this is so. First, the United Nations (UN) is a complex and multifaceted institution that carries out many roles in humanitarian relief by means of multiple organizations. However, the General Assembly has not designated a lead agency among these entities or provided one with full authority to coordinate and monitor the activities of the others. The United Nations High Commissioner for Refugees (UNHCR), UN Office for the Coordination of Humanitarian Affairs, UN Children's Education Fund, World Health Organization, and World Food Program, among others, may all be involved in any given crisis. None, however, enjoys an authoritative role to oversee its peers. None can require that other participating units undertake specific actions. Consequently, the UN response to humanitarian crises is fractionated organizationally along functional lines (Kent, 1987; Borton, 1993).

This institutional and managerial complexity is not the least of the obstacles to effective humanitarian coordination. The variety of UN agencies that may be deployed in crises is matched by the fact that a host of international nongovernmental organizations (INGOs), intranational nongovernmental organizations (NGOs), and state actors are also likely to be engaged in specific relief events. These organizations all strive to provide direct aid and capacity building to those affected by crises.

Another way to frame this issue is simply to say that the implementation environment of humanitarian emergencies includes a variety of actors, each operating under different constraints. No one of the various UN relief agencies enjoys a mandate (and a secure budget) to ensure coordination among them. INGOs, as separate organizational actors with their own missions, face similar financial uncertainty and in any case also lack a common overseer. Local NGOs may also be actively involved in the provision of aid, and these organizations, by definition, are likely to vary widely in organizational legitimacy and fiscal and managerial capacity. Forces deployed by other nations, as well as those of the affected state, may be involved, and the reasons for their engagement may differ little

Studies of humanitarian aid delivery have routinely concluded that these complex crises provide an inhospitable setting for coordination.

or sharply from those of other primary actors (as their sponsors elect). To complicate matters still further, if the disaster is linked to war or internal conflict, the local government's capacity and political will to act may be severely limited ("Fleeing the Horsemen Who Kill for Khartoum," 2004).

The plurality of aid organizations involved in relief delivery suggests that the strategic context for top-down coordination is likely to be inauspicious. Competing missions, differing organizational strategies, policies, and norms, as well as funding mandates make it difficult for the leaders of this complex array of relief institutions to focus on matters (interorganizational coordination) that seem to lie beyond their own organizational reach (Scott, 2003). In addition, relationships among UN organizations, INGOs, and NGOs often create subnetworks of action that complicate the humanitarian aid delivery structure even further. Operating authority in this decentralized and multiorganizational structure is shared among a number of related but at least quasi-autonomous participants.

Relief Aid Structures as Interorganizational Networks

In 1991 the United Nations established the Department of Humanitarian Affairs, later named the Office for the Coordination of Humanitarian Affairs (OCHA). Its mandate includes "the coordination of humanitarian response, policy development and humanitarian advocacy" (United Nations Office for the Coordination of Humanitarian Affairs, 2005). Despite its charge, OCHA does not enjoy command and control authority over the many UN entities often engaged in humanitarian relief, let alone over the other organizations involved in these emergencies (Reindorp and Wiles, 2001). As Larry Minear, a leading researcher in this field, has remarked, "In my judgment, the continuing absence of effective coordination structures remains the soft underbelly of the humanitarian enterprise" (2002, p. 21). While sharing the view that the UN designate an agency to provide authority over the players in the field, he recognizes that this proposition is arguable and that neither the various UN organizations nor the key donor nations have thus far assented to it. Indeed, he has suggested that they have actively resisted it.

Given that the complexity of aid delivery and the contested role of potential leaders make centralized control unlikely, perhaps there is a different way to conceptualize the challenges these complex implementation structures represent (Ring, 1997). Rather than continue to contend that the existing organization of humanitarian actors should conform with a principal-agent view of organizational coordination, it might be useful to conceive of humanitarian organizations engaged in relief work as engaged in an implementation network and seek to build some common set

The plurality of aid organizations involved in relief delivery suggests that the strategic context for top-down coordination is likely to be inauspicious.

of claims on that basis. O'Toole (1997) has offered a relevant definition of networks:

> Networks are structures of interdependence involving multiple organizations or parts thereof, where one unit is not merely the formal subordinate of the other in some larger hierarchical arrangement. Networks exhibit some structural stability but extend beyond formal established linkages and policy legitimated ties. The notion of networks excludes more formal hierarchies and perfect markets, but includes a wide range of structures in between. The institutional glue congealing networked ties may include authority bonds, exchange relations and coalitions based on common interest, all within a single multiunit structure. [p. 45]

The humanitarian scenario is one of diffuse authority among a range of players unwilling . . . to cede controlling authority of organizational action to any other single network player.

No formal hierarchy exists among humanitarian aid actors. Indeed, the primary glue that may be said to bind the diverse organizations involved in relief efforts together is their common interest in providing aid. Each may also perhaps be said to share an interest in developing some (contestable) norms of how relief should be delivered. Beyond these potentials, such coordination as occurs is (re)created with each new crisis situation.

The humanitarian scenario is one of diffuse authority among a range of players unwilling, for a variety of often cogent reasons—competition for media salience, competition for resources, fragmented missions, perceived national interests, among others—to cede controlling authority of organizational action to any other single network player (Borton, 1993). The operational challenge therefore lies not in finding means to persuade UN members or INGOs or NGOs to provide for more centralized strategic-level coordination and control of their actions or in seeking to overcome the deficiencies of coordination by consensus, but in devising humanitarian social networks of action that can act effectively without such central control or direction. This requires organizational networks in which stakeholders develop a robust array of communication channels that foster interorganizational awareness and trust (Hattori and Lapidus, 2004). Trust may be the lubricant for interorganizational action, but it is clear that it is not automatically extended or renewed once lost (Dirks and Ferrin, 2001). It is also clear that trust alone is not likely to be sufficient to secure coordination. Trust may well may exist between organizations or specific professionals in different organizations and not prove so strong as other competing organizational or professional claims.

Methodology

To begin to explore empirically the utility of this conceptualization of relief efforts, we conducted lengthy open-ended interviews with a small sample ($N = 5$) of experienced INGO professionals and leaders who were deployed in the Kosovo region in the late summer of 1999. Each individual interviewed worked for a different INGO. We tape-recorded and transcribed each interview. On average, each session lasted about ninety to one hundred minutes. Respondents, whose professional experience averaged fifteen years each, provided their insights into patterns of interinstitutional trust building, boundary-spanning behavior (why an individual would choose to work with someone in another organization), and coordination in that crisis. We recognize that our sample, indeed the Kosovo aid scenario itself, is not representative, if such a thing as a representative relief experience may even be said to exist. Nevertheless, this approach enabled us to contextualize our research with thick descriptions even as it allowed us, however tentatively, to begin exploring the dynamics that underpin the development and extension of trust across organizational boundaries in relief scenarios. INGOs often interact with virtually all other organizational players in these complex structures. As a result, our observers were well positioned to help us understand more thoroughly the dynamics of these efforts.

Our interviews also shed light on some possible ways more effective aid agency coordination might be achieved.

We sought to use our interviews to understand the context in which such choices were made and the role that trust played in professionals' decisions to seek or agree to coordination. Our respondents requested that we keep their identities confidential. Thus, all names used here are fictitious. We have retained transcripts in a secure location should there ever be reason to ask interviewees to divulge their identities. As we began, we postulated, as the relevant literature has argued, that trust is essential to boundary spanning between organizations and that such bridging behavior is essential to effective interorganizational coordination (Noteboom and Six, 2003).

Kosovo 1999

The history of the Kosovo crisis has been well treated elsewhere (for example, Minear, 2002). We provide a capsule description of events leading up to the crisis and a depiction of humanitarian aid deployment to address it. This analysis is followed by a consideration of factors, as identified by our INGO interviewees, of conditions that either fostered or hampered humanitarian aid coordination, including the role of UN donor nations. These insights provide a basis for understanding the challenges of aid delivery coordination in context, as well some clues concerning the role of trust in interorganizational relationships. Our interviews also shed light on some possible ways more effective aid agency coordination might be achieved. Or, perhaps better put, they help to paint a more thorough portrait of the nature of the coordination challenge.

On June 25, 1991, Slovenia and Croatia declared independence from the Socialist Federal Republic of Yugoslavia. Slovenia broke free without incident, but the situation in Croatia escalated into a war between Croatia's Serb minority and its majority ethnic Croat population. Similarly, in April 1992, Bosnia-Herzegovina declared its independence. The resultant conflict there found ethnic Serbs, Croats, and Muslims at war (Young, 2001). Whatever the origins of these conflicts, each shortly became a struggle for territory, with human displacement a central aim of several of the principal combatants.

The initial international community response to these events was to offer humanitarian aid rather than to intervene militarily. At the local level, "the parties to the conflict regarded the humanitarian players as protagonists in the political process" (Young, 2001, p. 788). Since siege and starvation were weapons of the war, "the delivery of humanitarian relief was not seen as a neutral humanitarian act" (Young, 2001, p. 789). The preventive protection policy of the UNHCR directly contradicted the displacement aims of the warring factions. It was therefore difficult for that agency, as well as other INGOs and NGOs, to intervene neutrally to provide humanitarian aid—at least as the antagonists perceived matters.

Our respondents worked in Kosovo to address the humanitarian aid crisis that arose in the wake of the NATO bombings there in spring 1999. The bombings, carried out to end what had become an especially cruel and brutal ethnic conflict, paradoxically created a severe refugee crisis. Aid organizations deployed to deliver food, shelter, and medical assistance to those refugees. Strong media coverage focused international attention on the crisis, thus increasing the amount of funding distributed among aid organizations willing to work in the theater. Our interviewees reported an intense agglomeration and proliferation of aid delivery organizations in the region within a very short period. According to one of our respondents, Linden, "In August, there were already somewhere around 200 organizations, 250 organizations. By September or October, there was something like 500. . . . It was just unbelievable."

The Kosovo aid situation was overseen by UNHCR for the UN, which disbursed funds and held sector-specific meetings among organizations receiving funding—health, water and sanitation, education, housing and infrastructure, and so on—aimed at securing increased cooperation and coordination among them. In addition to INGOs receiving support through UNHCR, there were independent INGOs of varying size, faith-based INGOs, and various NGOs and for-profit organizations operating in country—all with the avowed aim of providing emergency humanitarian relief. There was no local government in place immediately following the bombings, and no umbrella organization of local NGOs aimed at coordinating their efforts existed either.

Trust and Coordination in Kosovo

The aid situation in Kosovo evidenced relationships among actors on several levels. First, there was a network of principals through which aid funding flowed. In this case, state actors—the United States and the European Union, for example—provided funding for projects separately, as well as via the UN through UNHCR. Second, a core group of INGOs operated in the theater. These organizations tend to provide aid in virtually all major aid emergencies and include the International Rescue Committee, Oxfam, CARE, Worldvision, Americare, and Doctors Without Borders. These institutions are well known to the various UN aid agencies, to major state donors, and to one another. Each enjoys a reputation for special capacity in aid delivery in particular sectors (health, food, shelter, sanitation). In addition to this group, other INGOs and for-profit entities were present in Kosovo. Last, among the organizational actors, veteran relief workers formed interpersonal networks with staff of other organizations with whom they had served previously.

A network approach allows the analyst to focus on a number of important dimensions of humanitarian aid delivery (Ring, 1997). Network structures are uniquely adaptive to highly complex situations characterized by crisis and change. Research on networks "focuses on relations and patterns of relations rather than on [the] attributes of actors" (organizations), although analysts recognize the interdependence of these factors. In addition, networks may be examined at multiple levels or scales of analysis (Kilduff and Tsai, 2003, p. 19).

Our interviews suggest that different mechanisms for trust and coordination correspond with each of the analytical levels at which interactions occur among the array of organizations in the relief network. At the organizational scale, funding through the UN provided both incentive and at least a potential mechanism for cooperation; however, that incentive (largely the implicit threat of a loss of funding) was often either not present in practice (the UN lacked sufficient capacity or will, or both, to deliver the services in lieu of the organizations with which it was contracting) or not determinative (for organizations with independent sources of funds, including support from specific nations or multilaterals).

Different forms of information sharing aimed at coordination occurred at different levels in the network as well (Williams, 2002). In Kosovo, for example, UNHCR hosted NGO coordinating council and sectoral meetings that provided a means for understanding what each organization was doing, and who the other actors in the relief network were: "Especially at the beginning, there were a lot of meetings to basically carve out, you know, the sectors and the problems and say, okay, well you will do this in [city] and we will do X in [city], and that's the way we're going to divide it to make sure that everybody gets a piece of the pie" (Jackson).

Our respondents, all veterans of many emergency relief efforts, characterized these meetings as generally helpful, but that helpfulness came with certain drawbacks: "There were so many coordination meetings; if I'm not mistaken, there were a dozen a day for different sectors. But the major ones which happened would often

A network approach allows the analyst to focus on a number of important dimensions of humanitarian aid delivery.

involve a hundred-plus people sitting in a room and somebody would just call out security information, and so there wasn't any real, shared objective. . . . So I think that that would also help to build trust, if you knew why you were going there and you had a common objective" (Lin).

As this observation suggests, the most significant value of these meetings was the networking opportunities they presented: "It wasn't so much about coordination, I think, as much as it was about information sharing" (Jackson). "Usually you go for, you meet some people, and at that meeting nothing happens. But maybe three weeks down the line, something is coming up . . . you say, 'Oh yeah, I met that guy there . . . remember that guy say he was in this?' and that's how it happens. So, it's . . . as a matter of fact, when you look at the general meetings, you can see they are useful because people complain about it, but they are still coming" (Linden).

At the organizational level, the main basis for trust, a sine qua non of willingness to work across organizational boundaries and therefore of coordination, appears to be a multifaceted view of reputation, based both on the standing and mission of the organization with which an individual is affiliated and on past personal and professional interaction with that person (Williams, 2002). Our respondents indicated that they relied on knowledge of the organization's reputation for service delivery in particular sectors, as well as perceptions of their experience (and that of others they trusted in their own organizations) with that institution in prior crises: "I trusted UNHCR or another organization if I felt that I could rely on what they were telling me, that their information was valid" (Jackson).

At the organizational level, the main basis for trust . . . appears to be a multifaceted view of reputation.

In addition to prior knowledge or experience with other organizations or individuals working in them, respondents placed a strong emphasis on other organizational factors when determining whether to trust and therefore cooperate with representatives of other institutions. An organization's mission, for example, and its reputation and capacity for carrying out that mission as it sought to address a specific humanitarian emergency also shaped views of trustworthiness. "I go to an intervention like Kosovo with the purpose of helping the community to overcome the situation they are facing, and the trust I will put in other organizations would be their capacity in country to support that mission with their own intervention" (Linden).

Common organizational values were another basis for extending trust. Perhaps not surprisingly, interviewees found it easier to trust other organizational representatives when their stated aims were similar. Other characteristics, such as complementary competencies, also caused participants to view coordination more positively and to be more likely to trust other organization incumbents than they would have otherwise. "I would say it's around clarity, in terms of different roles and responsibilities. It's respect for each other's particular competencies, and it's a confidence in each other that we will act consistently in the best interest of those who we seek to help" (Hannaford).

In short, given the large number of actors and the pressure for rapid service delivery, respondents relied heavily on a reputation decision heuristic that connoted trustworthiness and operated at both organizational and individual scales when deciding when and with whom to cooperate across organizational lines. When devoting attention to the provision of key services, there is often simply not time to develop professional relationships with new or unknown actors; therefore, knowledge of an organization and established perceptions of its competence become a method for deciding with whom to coordinate. Given the deluge of responsibilities and the limited time in which to address them, willingness to coordinate is often determined by pre-existing network paths such as those that exist among a core group of INGO professionals whose organizations, operations, and even professional reputations are well known to one another.

Our respondents also suggested that aid delivery is strongly shaped by personal relationships. At the interpersonal level, respondents reported that personalities and perceived professional competence and relationships were key to effective coordination. "If I have a choice, I will pick up somebody I like. If I don't have a choice, and I need that service, the community needs that service, well, I will go along with that organization providing that their professionalism and their resources are adequate" (Linden).

Such relationships are embedded within the context of aid delivery and may be conveyed from country to country, crisis to crisis. Indeed, some respondents explicitly relied on a network of contacts in Kosovo. "I mean, sometimes you go to places like [country] and it's like drowning, you know, everybody you've ever known in your life for the last fifteen years passes before your eyes, and nobody's surprised to see each other. And that—good personal relationships—are actually fundamental to that" (Hannaford).

A reputation heuristic, in this case one developed on the basis of prior experience with an individual in a crisis intervention, appears to play a significant role in individual willingness to trust others in different organizations to work with them and to cooperate in the provision of services. "You know, when people ask you, well, you know, where were you before, or how many years you have been doing this, and you kind of think, to sort of establish your credibility and how much they can trust you" (Jackson).

Organization reputation and perceived professional competence trump personal relationships in the absence of such knowledge, but personal knowledge, when it exists, may be critical to decisions to extend trust and therefore to cooperate across organization lines. Aid workers may be skeptical or even jaundiced about a specific organization, but if they believe their counterpart there is competent and trustworthy, they are likely to agree to coordinate anyway. These relationships are self-reinforcing; good reputations and experience in one theater make it more likely that harmonization of activities will occur in future scenarios, a sort of self-fulfilling prophecy.

Good reputations and experience in one theater make it more likely that harmonization of activities will occur in future scenarios.

In addition, interorganizational relationships are often shaped significantly by role equivalence, that is, among actors who play similar roles within different organizations (Perrone, Zaheer, and McEvily, 2003). "Quite often it's easy, if not easier, for people with a common technical background and skill and discipline to form relationships among their counterparts" (Hannaford).

Organizational representatives describe a situation in which relationships at the interorganizational (network), organizational, and interpersonal levels play a major role in coordination. This finding supports previous findings (Friedman and Podolny, 1992). Each of these scales constitutes a piece of the network of humanitarian aid delivery, of which single organizations are only a part. The existence of these networks strongly influences how organizations behave in country. Given the variability of preexisting organizational and individual (personal and professional) ties and varying crisis situations, we turn next to a discussion of the factors particular to organizations that might encourage or discourage coordination.

Funding and Coordination

If funding can operate as an organizationally exogenous or strategic-scale variable, the source of funding can also act as an organizational-level incentive that conditions whether institutions participate in coordination efforts. If an organization relies primarily on private and dedicated funding sources, it may have no incentive to cooperate with other institutions. Many of our respondents observed that they were familiar with organizations acting as lone wolves. These actors operate outside of networks, and the independent character of their funding ultimately shapes how aid is delivered since many feel no imperative to coordinate their efforts with other organizations in the network. "If you've got your own independent funding, why there's no pressure on you, nobody can really pressure you into collaborating. And typically quite a few of those individuals and people show up, but a lot of them are hustlers. I mean, some of them are very good, but a lot of them are hustlers who make big promises and then disappear" (Grimes).

Private funders (like public ones) may place restrictions on the type of aid delivered. This leads some organizations to provide services only so long as funding lasts. "This is a problem with a lot of smaller, mostly faith-based agencies, or agencies coming from countries that don't have a lot of experience doing humanitarian work, who would go into different villages and say that they were going to work on a project, and you know, start the project, and then, you know, run out of funds in the middle of it and leave it there. . . . And of course they hadn't coordinated with anybody" (Jackson).[1] Since whether to accept funding lies within each organizational actor's purview, the funding source may act within organizations to condition their willingness to coordinate with other entities.

Organizational type can also play a role in organizational choice making concerning coordination. For-profit organizations are beginning to emerge as aid contractors. Our respondents found for-profits to be highly competitive in their behavior in relation to other relief providers. "I think this new environment where the for-profits are playing a larger role probably discourages information sharing . . . a lot of NGOs have gotten a little bit burned by for-profits coming and using a lot of information and then not giving you any, or actually using it to go and get a huge contract" (Jackson).

Our interviewees suggested that for-profits did not give much thought to holistic service delivery or capacity building, although their delivery could be characterized as efficient. The profit motive may not encourage coordination with other organizations or aid recipients. "[For-profits want to] get the job done and make some money doing it, and NGOs wouldn't be quite as mercenary, but they would want to do the job right. They wouldn't just want to put a school on the ground. They would want to make sure that local folks built it, and there was a teacher, and there were schoolbooks, and you would hope that they would do a more rounded package beyond what a contractor might do" (Grimes).

Our interviewees suggested that for-profits did not give much thought to holistic service delivery or capacity building.

Many other factors, including staff training and composition, are clearly within the control of organizations and influence service delivery choices and strategies. Staff training shapes how prepared relief organizations are to act within their missions to deliver services and cope with a crisis environment. Representatives of the large INGOs emphasize coordination and stress that in their staff retention and development programs. Organizations also control the mix of staff, combining experienced and inexperienced employees such that the latter can be drawn into existing networks: "If individual organizations are responsible around the blend of experience and innovation and bringing people on within their team, then it means that you can actually bring to the table a whole wealth of prior organizational relationships" (Hannaford). However, the rapid deployment of assistance in Kosovo resulted in understaffing, as well as problems with inexperienced people on the ground, that is, with "individuals within the organizations not being aware of their organizational mandates, organizational history, and also not being fully aware of the context of the Kosovo crisis" (Lin).

Viewing Kosovo through a network lens points up aspects of coordination that lie beyond the control of any single organizational actor. Indeed, a complex structure of interorganizational relationships exists in virtually any conceivable crisis-aid situation. But it cannot be said that such structures are static from crisis to crisis. This is so because not only do organizational incentives and personnel change, but so too does the strategic context to which both organizations and individuals react and in which they are inevitably enmeshed. The context of humanitarian crises and the impact of that context on the network of organizations carry implications for whether and to what extent coordination may occur (Wicks and Berman, 2004).

Strategic Structure of the Humanitarian Network Operating Environment

We have argued that humanitarian aid delivery networks evince relatively weak but enduring structural ties. This is so because a common cast of actors—UN agencies and major INGOs—typically responds when humanitarian crises erupt. However, the context of each crisis differs, presenting challenges to coordination and cooperation even among network actors that are otherwise aware of one another's activities and strengths and weaknesses. Among the contextual factors are these:

Many strategic conditions contributed to the chaotic organizational environment of aid delivery in Kosovo. Chief among these was media attention.

- Local capacity—the stability of government in the affected nation as well as its will and ability to respond
- Financial resources available at the national and international levels
- The response of the United Nations—military, humanitarian, or both—in the context of civil conflict[2]
- Character and capacity of the leadership of relevant UN, INGO, governmental, and local actors

Our interviewees indicated that factors such as media salience, funding, interorganizational competition, stress, and the unfolding of events on the ground also had a profound impact on the coordination of aid delivery in Kosovo. We discuss these issues further.

Media Salience

Many strategic conditions contributed to the chaotic organizational environment of aid delivery in Kosovo. Chief among these was media attention, which influenced the amount of available funding and led to a comparatively large level of service organization deployment. Cooley and Ron (2002) have characterized the aid delivery scenario as innately highly competitive. Our respondents agree, indicating that funding created a large pool of actors, all vying for available contracts. The rapid rise in the number of organizations in country created a chaotic environment. One of the characteristics of that environment was competition: "There's always that competition. I mean, I was certainly guilty of it in Kosovo, you know, and I competed with a lot of agencies and made sure I got my proposals in there first, so that I would get the money and not the others. You know, we all want to be able to say that our NGO is doing the most work, or the best work, and I think that's part of human nature" (Jackson). Another characteristic was a narrow focus on the task at hand: "People weren't sure what others were doing, there were simply too many NGOs, and the pressures of running your organization, running your program and meeting media and dollar demands meant that people very quickly found niches to operate in, and that then stopped the consultation process, or the sharing process between NGOs, but more importantly, between NGOs and beneficiaries" (Lin). "As a result of that, we worked twelve hours a day, seven days a week, and if you were coming to my office and say 'you know, I need to coordinate, or this or this,' right now, with crisis after crisis after crisis, I don't have the time or the mind, I don't have the mind, to just talk about coordination, you see what I mean?" (Linden).

Stress and Timing

In part due to the large number of actors in the theater, several respondents characterized Kosovo as among the most highly stressful aid interventions in which they had participated: "It wasn't just the pressure of the work and the media and the donors, but also the living conditions were pretty bad. It was one of the worst winters in history, and there was no heat, no hot water, and no electricity, and so, you know, you would be putting in twelve hours at work and then going home to a cold apartment that you couldn't heat properly, and it made it very difficult for people to cope with the circumstances" (Jackson).

One compared Kosovo to less stressful situations and pointed to stages of the intervention that were more or less conducive to coordination: "I will take the example of [country], as being the other extreme for me; [it] was probably my best experience over the last ten years I spent overseas. And the reason was it was a small community of NGOs. I think when we had general meetings, you could put us around the dining room table, it was something like seven or eight organizations. . . . As a result of that . . . the level of coordination there was something I never experienced before or since" (Linden).

Linden's comment also illustrates several dimensions of the context of relief network coordination dynamics. To use a democratic analogy, it is difficult to manage democratic participation among large numbers of agents. The ability to coordinate ultimately may be related to the number of actors or entities involved. The problem is how to know when the threshold of "too many" is reached and what might be done when it is attained. The complexity of humanitarian relief structures should, at the least, elicit a certain modesty of expectations for widespread coordination among the many parties. In addition, the capacity of the various participants to coordinate is clearly shaped fundamentally by the level of stress in a given scenario, a strategic factor that is beyond the purview of any one organization or group of organizations. Stress appears to work against fulsome coordination. Harmonization may be more possible at various stages of an intervention. Early stages featuring intense world attention, high funding levels, and many actors may not be as conducive to coordination as later stages. Ironically, when stress and emotionally pervasive urgency are reduced, interorganizational coordination may be more possible and broader ranging.

Media attention, funding cycles, and organizational competition may also have an unfortunate impact on service recipients. Funding, for example, can determine whether an adequate level of humanitarian assistance is available for a given crisis situation. "Everybody likes to work in Thailand, for example. . . . The joke in Thailand is, you know, every NGO's got its own refugee. But you go over to Bangladesh, and you don't find that many of them . . . so there tends to be a disproportionate amount of aid going into some areas—the more comfortable, nice areas—and less aid going into other areas that might be equally or even more needy" (Grimes). "The number of organizations was due to funding availability, the media attention, and a subset to that is the fact that this was the first big crisis, the first very big publicized crisis where the beneficiaries were all white. And there was . . . proximity to places where there were a lot of charitable organizations" (Lin).

Perversely, too much cash available in too short a time frame can interfere with effective aid delivery and with coordination.

Funding restrictions may actually mediate against capacity building among service recipients. In effect, funding may create a condition in which recipients are excluded from networks. Perversely, too much cash available in too short a time frame can interfere with effective aid delivery and with coordination. In Kosovo, a great deal of aid flowed in a very limited period (roughly ninety days), and the result was increased competition among aid organizations and less willingness to coordinate activities with potential recipients. The UN, bilateral organizations, and INGOs may not be as open to citizens and NGOs in country as one might imagine. "There was a great deal of provision of services without any consultation . . . whether it was what the people really wanted or prioritized themselves, and people's lack of involvement in implementation of services, I mean, beneficiaries' lack of involvement" (Lin). "In Kosovo, you have no NGO leaders of a sector meeting. They were always from some big international organization. And that kind of disenfranchised them, I think" (Linden).

Funding availability may provide incentives to harmonize, but it may also operate against coordination. Money alone is not a sufficient condition to ensure that individual actors will elect to span organizational boundaries and work with representatives of other organizations to secure coordination, or to secure organization-to-organization boundary spanning either (Noteboom and Six, 2003).

One large barrier to developing capacity is the pay structure of international aid organizations. "The Kosovar government, the new Kosovar government after the Serbs were thrown out, after the war, after the refugees came back, paid about $100 to doctors. So, doctors were going to work for the UN as chauffeurs at $400 a month. And this is typical. The UN grabs the best of the people, or USAID grabs the best of the people because they pay the best salaries. The NGOs get the second best because they pay the second best salaries. And the government, that your overriding objective in the country is to create a viable government, gets nothing" (Grimes).

The network of humanitarian aid is thus conditioned by strategic factors present in the crisis situation itself. Competition, media attention, funding levels and timing, and the intensity of the crisis can all influence the ability and willingness of network actors to coordinate across organizational lines. These factors may even operate at some points to exclude some groups, including aid recipients and NGOs, from their rightful roles in coordination efforts since these parties are often new to other actors, may evidence relatively weak or evolving capacities, and are "untested."

Whither Humanitarian Relief Coordination?

A contextualized view of aid delivery in humanitarian crises illustrates the complexity as well as the barriers to coordination across organizational lines. In our view, we should be modest in our expectations about how quickly and completely interorganizational structures of this size and complexity may be expected to respond to calls for increased coordination. Our respondents offered many insights regarding how to improve the likelihood of improved harmonization in relief networks. First, many were skeptical of centralized coordination through UNHCR, UNOCHA, ECHO, or any other UN entity. Significantly, as a group, their level of trust of these entities was limited: "UNHCR certainly didn't work; there was very little mutual trust within that" (Hannaford). "I had some difficulties at one point with UNHCR, and part of it stems from the fact that, that it was difficult to get reliable information from them, that they would tell you one thing one day, and another one the next. . . . Also, different people within the organization were telling you different things. So, that made it very, very difficult for a while to actually be able to have a really meaningful and trusting working relationship with them" (Jackson).

This is not to suggest that more centralized forms of coordination are impossible. Rather, it implies that further exploration of network dynamics is needed to discover the types of leadership and forms of information sharing that would be most effective in this complex set of relationships. At the least, one may not simply assume the efficacy of a principal-agent set of relationships or simple command-and-control approach.

As an alternative, many of our respondents believed that coordination might well be improved by means of a nonhierarchical, network-type response. In this view, INGO and NGO representatives themselves could assume a leadership role in coordination. "In many cases, the United Nations is not in a good position at all to coordinate the work of NGOs. The NGOs themselves, and perhaps with civil society, would be in a better position to self-manage their activities, to self-regulate their work, and, the UN being as it is, inevitably highly politicized, highly bureaucratic, not in all cases but generally I would say, and also having many, many other agendas, but also not necessarily understanding . . . NGO workers and NGO agendas" (Lin). "But national and . . . international organizations . . . are core groups that are very well known from the donor, and they are well known to each other because they work together, and that could be put in a role of leadership. And I'm not saying that there aren't issues with leadership in every country, because we do not have that capacity in every country, but there are countries where we are able to be the leadership role" (Linden).

Such an approach, however, would need to have a strong foundation of shared values and standards as these underpin decisions among professionals to extend trust across organizational boundaries to secure improved coordination (Benini, 1997). Several of our respondents noted that aid delivery has improved markedly in the years since Kosovo, largely due to the development of service and professional standards by a number of groups: "I think there's been a sort of a quantum leap in the last four years, five years, in organizations understanding the need for standards, minimum standards in the work they do, particularly in service positions, and in particular Sphere standards and similar internal standards which have been developed by MSF [Médecins sans Frontières] or other organizations" (Lin). "The Good Donorship Initiative . . . meets a couple of times a year; it's basically a set-up of major humanitarian aid donors, and they've gotten together and put together some, I think, common codes or principles which they are promoting" (Lin).

The adoption and integration of a set of common standards among a changing and diverse network of organizations and entities is hardly a sure thing.

Organizations themselves, recognizing the need for better coordination, are embracing such standards as well as developing their own. While developing policies, practices, and values at the organizational level is certainly feasible, the adoption and integration of a set of common standards among a changing and diverse network of organizations and entities is hardly a sure thing, and there is no obvious path for the transmission of such standards among "lone wolves," those organizations with no obvious incentive to coordinate. Furthermore, such an approach depends heavily on an honor system among organizations and on strong mission identification and training within organizations because of the highly dynamic nature of crisis intervention.

Figure 1 summarizes a number of the contextual factors we have discussed and suggests how each helps shape the potential for coordination at different levels of analysis and of organizational action. The extension of trust at least partially mediates these potentials at all levels of analysis. First, at the macrostrategic level, it seems clear that nations and national policy choices shape all else in the humanitarian environment. If key countries elect not to respond to a crisis or to do so half-heartedly, the consequences for all that follows are profound. The tepid American response to the Rwanda and Darfur genocides may provide examples (Dallaire, 2004; Hatzfeld, 2005). These state calculations are not solely the products of trust or its dearth, but instead the consequences of multiple factors, including

Figure 1. Contextual Factors and Their Effect on Coordination Potential

Operative Levels of Trust	Contextual Factors				
	Interpersonal Contacts / Reputation	Funding	Inter-organizational Competition	Media Salience	Stress of Relief Work
Strategic	Pre-existing network paths; common cast of actors	High funding levels supporting many actors not as conducive to coordination at later stages	For-profit aid contractors less likely to coordinate	Media attention influences amount of available funding and may lead to large level of service organization deployment in short time frames	Capacity to coordinate beyond purview of any one organization
	Character and capacity of leadership of relevant UN, INGO, governmental, and local actors	Number of organizations related to funding availability	Funding creates a large pool of actors vying for available contracts	Harmonization possible at early stages with world attention	Reduced stress and urgency promotes interorganizational coordination
	Many actors skeptical of centralized coordination	Funding restrictions mediate against capacity building among service recipients	Ability to coordinate related to number of actors or entities involved		
	Strong foundation of shared values and standards required for trust and boundary spanning	Too much funding within a short time frame at early stages can interfere with effective aid delivery and coordination	Response of UN: whether and how		
Organizational	Complementary competencies between organizations	Potential mechanism for cooperation; incentive (threat of loss of funding)			
	Knowledge of service delivery in particular sectors; standing and capacity for carrying out mission	Resources available at national and international levels	Pay structure of international aid organizations competes with UN or USAID for the best staff		
	"Untested" actors may be excluded		Local capacity; stability of government and its will and ability to respond		
	Shared service and professional standards improve aid delivery				
Individual	Past personal and professional interaction; role equivalence	Funding alone not sufficient to ensure that individual actors will span organizational boundaries	Staff training and core competencies		Inexperienced staff on the ground
	Perceptions of individual's experience with organization in prior crises				

Elements that promote trust and boundary spanning

protection of state sovereignty and perceived scope of action. Once an intervention is accepted, however, levels of interstate trust may indeed become more salient for coordination as key choices occur concerning funding and support levels. At the network level, meanwhile, the decision by member nations not to accord a single UN entity authority over relief efforts guarantees that the current clumsy international interorganizational humanitarian service structure will endure. That choice surely reflects, at least in part, the judgments of member nations about which organizations may be trusted and which not, even as it obviously reflects their collective desire to preserve wide discretion over how to react to humanitarian relief emergencies. Media salience matters to states strategically as they make these choices, at least to the extent that it may arouse their populations to demand a response. It appears, however, that such salience may make it more, not less, difficult for network participants to cooperate as it places enormous pressures on each to demonstrate its role and efficacy to its stakeholders.

Ultimately much of the potential for coordination rests with individual choices made by professionals in the field.

Trust appears significant at the organizational scale in at least two ways. First, it may help to establish shared organizational norms that, encouraged by similar missions or normative aspirations, may encourage organization-to-organization cooperation. Second, it may encourage individual professionals with knowledge of a counterpart in another organization to work across organizational boundaries and coordinate activities with that individual and, thereby, his or her organization. Meanwhile, it is important to recall that at the organization scale, factors such as competition for salience or funding may work against these possibilities.

Finally, in an important sense, individuals mediate many operating-level choices in relief operations. They can, if they so elect, reach across organizational boundaries even in the face of incentives not to do so, but at considerable cost. Conversely, individuals may also resist interorganizational cooperation even when their organizational leaders request such action. Ultimately much of the potential for coordination rests with individual choices made by professionals in the field. As we note above, these are partly the product of disposition and personality, partly of professional capacity, and partly of the individual's understanding of the incentives at play. For those who would encourage greater coordination of activities in interorganizational relief networks the challenge is to maximize the number and quality of incentives that encourage cooperation—as field-level professionals understand these.

Conclusion

Our interviews confirmed for us afresh what others have already observed: humanitarian aid efforts are fraught with competition and confusion. These conditions are part and parcel of the overall environment of relief delivery and cannot simply be fixed by means of a more thoroughgoing top-down coordination. Humanitarian aid implementation is better conceived as a network of actors enmeshed, in part, within a set of preexisting relationships, brought together by an emergency, but with no natural lines of authority existing among them. This suggests that coordination takes place within a relational network of more or less independent organizations (at least from one another).

Our respondents often reminded us, if a reminder was needed, of the stressful, complex environment of humanitarian assistance. The intense pressure of emergency intervention and the often competitive processes by which aid allocations are provided make an already difficult situation still more challenging. These conditions suggest that any sort of coordination will be difficult, but it does appear that a network form of organization ultimately may be more responsive to the turbulent and changing situation. The notion that polycentricity permits more innovative and more varied responses is not new, but it does appear to be operative in humanitarian relief efforts. Its twin may also be operative: polycentric implementation structures implicitly depend on their weakest links for their overall effectiveness. In situations of crisis and dire need, this reality, whatever its theoretic advantages, may not be permissible to the parties involved.

The noncentralized character of aid delivery suggests in turn that the factors that can improve trust and coordination in humanitarian relief networks do not rest with any single actor. Organizations can individually institute rules and standards but cannot control the behavior of other organizations. One promising alternative is the establishment of norms and standards, such as those developed by Sphere and the Good Donorship Initiative, in networks that include major INGOs and donors. These standards condition the behavior of numerous organizations in an effort to secure coordination through self-regulation. While they are only as strong as the common normative claims that sustain them, these standards do appear to be a reasonable and necessary, if not yet sufficient, response to the strategic and operational environment of humanitarian aid delivery.

We set out to explore with a small but experienced group of professionals (our respondents) a key hypothesis advanced in the literature: whether and how trust might play a role in securing improved coordination among the many participants providing services in humanitarian relief scenarios. We found it does, but in unexpectedly complex ways that befit and mirror the complexities of the operating environment in which such choices are made. We also found that decisions to extend trust and thereby to enable various degrees of coordination and cooperation among organizations were influenced by factors at play at multiple analytical levels and so are subject to the vagaries of network dynamics.

As many in the literature have argued, trust is surely the lubricant of interorganizational decisions to coordinate activities inasmuch as effective coordination implies a disciplining of one's own unfettered capacity to act as perceived desirable in order to take into account the needs, claims, and desires of others. Such choices demand trust, which may result from personal or professional perceptions and knowledge, or amalgams of both of these, and may occur primarily at the individual level. Alternately, in the absence of the relationships and knowledge necessary for personal judgments, relief professionals may nonetheless extend trust to their counterparts in other organizations on the basis of perceived organizational legitimacy and competence. In either case, individuals alone do not mediate such choices, which are instead the product of organizational expectations, operating routines, and a host of strategic factors as well as personal predilection. Trust may be vital to decisions to coordinate actions across organizational boundaries, but it is hardly autonomously determined and by itself is unlikely to prove sufficient to secure coordination. That fact, coupled with the complexity of the implementation structure through which humanitarian relief is delivered, leads us to conclude that we should conceive of such efforts as networks and to imagine ways in which we can secure goal and values awareness and complementarity (where possible) among relief organizations and professionals before each is ensconced in the hothouse conditions that are the stuff of humanitarian relief. We are heartened by the steps that have been taken in this direction in recent years by a variety of relevant professional groups and hope such dialogue continues, but these initiatives will be only as successful as their widespread adoption (that is, active acceptance) by individuals involved in the many roles related to humanitarian relief. The challenge is not dissimilar to that confronting any leader who would establish global norms of action. In any case, the relief coordination problem is not merely structural, and we can conceive of no simple organizational fix that will set matters right among so complex a group of actors. Informed dialogue does seem an appropriate first-order response.

The relief coordination problem is not merely structural, and we can conceive of no simple organizational fix that will set matters right among so complex a group of actors.

Humanitarian aid delivery networks appear often to operate to exclude indigenous NGOs and citizens, and thereby indirectly to thwart in-country capacity building. The frequent absence of national representatives in coordinating meetings and the reliance among network participants on known quantities appear to make it especially difficult to develop relationships and build the capacity of NGOs in country. This result appears to be the product, at least in part, of the self-reinforcing feedback loops that typify relationships among actors who work together in one crisis after another. That almost dialectical relationship is constructive in the sense that it may create boundary-spanning behavior among individuals based on trust but, paradoxically, may be accompanied by an important negative externality. The very "strangeness" or novelty of most NGOs may make it more difficult for those entities to gain legitimacy in the relief process, even when they possess the necessary capacities and domestic representativeness or legitimacy to play significant aid roles. We believe that this is an area in which the need for more robust forms of trust and boundary-spanning behavior is keenly felt. In our view, the dynamics of how such inclinations might be developed or encouraged among otherwise often disparate organizations and between professionals within them requires more thorough study.

Notes

1. While some pointed to smaller faith-based organizations as more likely to go it alone, respondents, when asked to elaborate, refused to generalize, affirming that there are many faith-based organizations that operate in "good faith" as well as many competent small organizations operating in the field.

2. The presence or absence of civil conflict changes the humanitarian environment profoundly. This is so because its presence often endangers the lives of humanitarian aid agents while making their already difficult responsibilities often impossible to prosecute. It is also the case, however, because such strife—ethnic cleansing, warlord genocide, and so on—may bring foreign troops, and when nations commit troops they are very likely to set the conditions for all forms of action, humanitarian or otherwise, while their troops are under duress. Such nations control the theater of action and may simply use their military resources to augment, if not eclipse, their civilian humanitarian aid counterparts. Civil conflict is important for itself but just as significant for the interventions it brings and the consequences those choices bring for humanitarian organizations.

MAX STEPHENSON JR. *is codirector of the Institute for Governance and Accountabilities, School of Public and International Affairs, Virginia Polytechnic Institute and State University, Blacksburg, Virginia.*

MARCY H. SCHNITZER *is a research associate at the Institute for Governance and Accountabilities, School of Public and International Affairs, Virginia Polytechnic Institute and State University, Blacksburg, Virginia.*

References

Baumgartner, F. R., and Jones, B. D. *Agendas and Instability in American Politics.* Chicago: University of Chicago Press, 1993.

Benini, A. "Uncertainty and Information Flows in Humanitarian Agencies." *Disasters,* 1997, *21* (4), 335–353.

Borton, J. "Recent Trends in the International Relief System." *Disasters,* 1993, *17* (3), 187–201.

Cooley, A., and Ron, J. "The NGO Scramble: Organizational Insecurity and the Political Economy of Transnational Action." *International Security,* 2002, *27* (1), 5–39.

Dallaire, R. *Shake Hands with the Devil: The Failure of Humanity in Rwanda.* New York: Carroll and Graf, 2004.

Dirks, K., and Ferrin, D. "The Role of Trust in Organizational Settings." *Organization Science,* 2001, *12* (4), 450–467.

"Fleeing the Horsemen Who Kill for Khartoum." *Economist,* May 15, 2004, pp. 21–23.

Friedman, R., and Polodny, J. "Differentiation of Boundary Spanning Roles: Labor Negotiations and Implications for Role Conflict." *Administrative Science Quarterly,* 1992, *37* (1), 28–47.

Hattori, R., and Lapidus. T. "Collaboration, Trust and Innovative Change." *Journal of Change Management,* 2004, *4* (2), 97–104.

Hatzfeld, J. *Machete Season: The Killers in Rwanda Speak.* New York: Farrar, Straus and Giroux, 2005.

Kent, R. C. *Anatomy of Disaster Relief: The International Network in Action.* London: Pinter, 1987.

Kilduff, M., and Tsai, W. *Social Networks and Organizations.* Thousand Oaks, Calif.: Sage, 2003.

Macrae, J., and Harmer, A. (eds.). *Humanitarian Action and the "Global War on Terror": A Review of Trends and Issues.* London: Overseas Development Institute, 2003.

Minear, L. *The Humanitarian Enterprise: Dilemmas and Discoveries.* Bloomfield, Conn.: Kumarian Press, 2002.

Noteboom, B., and Six, F. *The Trust Process in Organizations: Empirical Studies of the Determinants and the Process of Trust Development.* Northampton, Mass.: Edward Elgar, 2003.

O'Toole, L. J. "Treating Networks Seriously: Practical and Research-Based Agendas in Public Administration." *Public Administration Review,* 1997, *57* (1), 45–52.

Perrone, V., Zaheer, A., and McEvily, B. "Free to Be Trusted? Organizational Constraints on Trust in Boundary Spanners." *Organization Science,* 2003, *14* (4), 422–439.

Reindorp, N., and Wiles, P. *Humanitarian Coordination: Lessons from Recent Field Experience.* London: Office for the Coordination of Humanitarian Affairs, Overseas Development Institute, 2001.

Rey, F. "The Complex Nature of Actors in Humanitarian Action and the Challenge of Coordination." In Humanitarian Studies Unit, *Reflections on Humanitarian Action: Principles, Ethics and Contradictions.* London: Pluto Press, 2001.

Ring, P. S. "Processes Facilitating Reliance on Trust in Inter-Organizational Networks." In M. Ebers (ed.), *The Formation of Inter-Organizational Networks.* New York: Oxford University Press, 1997.

Scott, W. R. *Organizations: Rational, Natural, and Open Systems.* Upper Saddle River, N.J.: Prentice Hall, 2003.

Stephenson, M., Jr. "Making Humanitarian Relief Networks More Effective: Operational Coordination, Trust and Sense Making." *Disasters,* 2005, *29* (4), 337–350.

Stephenson, M., Jr. "Toward a Descriptive Model of Humanitarian Assistance Coordination." *Voluntas: The International Journal of Voluntary and Nonprofit Organizations,* 2006, *17* (1), 1–17.

Stockton, N. *Strategic Coordination in Afghanistan.* Kabul: Afghanistan Research and Evaluation Unit, 2002.

United Nations Office for the Coordination of Humanitarian Affairs. *A Brief History of OCHA.* http://ochaonline.un.org/webpage.asp?Nav=_about_en&Site=_about. 2005.

Van de Ven, A., and Walker, G. "The Dynamics of Inter-Organizational Coordination." *Administrative Science Quarterly,* 1984, *29,* 598–621.

Weick, K. "Educational Organizations as Loosely Coupled Systems." *Administrative Science Quarterly,* 1976, *21,* 1–19.

Wicks, A., and Berman, S. "The Effects of Context on Trust in Firm-Stakeholder Relationships: The Institutional Environment, Trust Creation and Firm Performance." *Business Ethics Quarterly,* 2004, *14* (1), 141–160.

Williams, P. "The Competent Boundary Spanner." *Public Administration,* 2002, *80* (1), 103–124.

Young, K. "UNHCR and ICRC in the Former Yugoslavia: Bosnia-Herzegovina." *International Review of the Red Cross,* 2001, *83* (843), 781–805.

For bulk reprints of this article, please call (201) 748-8789.

BOOK REVIEWS

Social Marketing and Advocacy

Roseanne M. Mirabella

Social Marketing in the 21st Century, by Alan R. Andreasen. Thousand Oaks, Calif.: Sage, 2006. 280 pp., $72.95 cloth, $36.95 paper.

THERE ARE ALMOST sixty marketing courses offered by graduate programs throughout the country focused specifically on marketing for nonprofit organizations. Marketing is most often offered as a stand-alone course with an exclusive focus on marketing skills and concepts. Several programs teach marketing in conjunction with other curricular topics such as public relations and communications, strategic planning, or fundraising and development. Within these courses, students learn about the utility of marketing skills and concepts in identifying audiences, creating positive public images, and attracting donors and volunteers. However, not one of the courses offered by graduate degree programs in colleges and universities combines marketing with the topics of advocacy and public policy.

All this is about to change, according to Alan R. Andreasen, a leader in the field of social marketing and a strong proponent of the applicability of marketing to the field of nonprofit management. He argues that the traditional approach to marketing with its focus on downstream targets is too narrow in scope and needs to be repositioned to encompass both upstream and downstream approaches to social change. In fact, the goal of *Social Marketing in the 21st Century* is to reposition social marketing to influence the behavior of individuals to quit smoking, lose weight, or exercise more *and* the behavior of other actors who need to act as well in order to address these social issues, such as elected officials, local school districts, zoning boards, and police officers. Changing the behavior of individuals requires the use of downstream approaches, while upstream approaches must be used to influence the behavior of other target audiences in the social issue environment who need to enact no smoking laws, or build more recreational facilities, or support nutritious lunch programs in schools.

Part One introduces the social marketing topic and its importance in influencing the behavior of both downstream and upstream

actors when addressing social problems. Chapter Two focuses on the eight stages of the social change life cycle:

Stage 1: Inattention to the problem
Stage 2: Discovery of the problem
Stage 3: Climbing the agenda
Stage 4: Outlining the choices
Stage 5: Choosing courses of action
Stage 6: Launching initial interventions
Stage 7: Reassessing and redirecting efforts
Stage 8: Achieving success, failure, or neglect

[Andreasen] argues that the traditional approach to marketing with its focus on downstream targets is too narrow in scope.

Those of us who teach within nonprofit management programs will notice the symmetry between these stages and the stages of the public policy process. This is where Andreasen's work has the most potential: in the applicability of social marketing concepts and tools to influencing the behavior of major actors in the policy process. To make it easier for us to understand the process, Andreasen focuses on the social issue of childhood obesity, illustrating the applicability of social marketing in each stage of the policy life cycle. The real-life problem of childhood obesity will not be solved by merely focusing on the downstream behavior of individual children, their parents, and their siblings. Other actors must take action to fight childhood obesity, including school officials, health care workers, editors and reporters, television programmers, social service workers, nonprofit leaders, restaurant managers, fast-food industry leaders, food manufacturers, community planners, legislators, and regulators, all players in the public policy process.

Part Two shows how to use social marketing to bring a social problem through the various stages, focusing on the structure of a social problem, identifying the problem, and analyzing the various ways in which the problem might be addressed. Chapter Four discusses the role of social marketing in addressing target audiences at different points in the process. When deciding whether to change their behavior, target audiences must decide if they want to act and if they have the ability to act. The author proposes a framework to identify the factors motivating individuals to act:

• Benefits (motivators)
• Costs (demotivators)
• Others (either motivators or demotivators)
• Self-assurance (perceptions of opportunity and ability)

The remainder of the book (Parts Three and Four) focuses on upstream applications: influencing the behavior of local community members, influencing lawmakers and regulators, and creating alliances with business managers and members of the media. These sections are rich with examples of social marketing applications for approaching elected officials, local bureaucrats, members of the media, and corporate leaders. Chapter Eight discusses bringing about structural change in business practices to "promote the social good" (p. 170). The author shows us how to use the motivating factors to move individuals within corporations forward through the stages of the social change life cycle.

This book is a must-read for nonprofit managers and leaders who are interested in producing social change. The book would be a good primary text for a graduate or undergraduate course in nonprofit marketing. It would also do well as one of several books within a graduate course on public policy and advocacy. Andreasen successfully shows how the concepts and tools of social marketing can be used to influence the behavior not only of those downstream to the social problem but of those upstream as well. The social change life cycle framework provides a useful juxtaposition to the policy process model and can provide an excellent springboard for conversations among future nonprofit leaders on the appropriate role of advocacy, lobbying, and social marketing in the nonprofit setting.

> *This book is a must-read for nonprofit managers and leaders who are interested in producing social change.*

ROSEANNE M. MIRABELLA is an associate professor in the Political Science Department at Seton Hall University, South Orange, New Jersey. She has been tracking the development of nonprofit management education and philanthropy programs since 1995, creating and maintaining the Web site that currently houses the database (http://pirate.shu.edu/~mirabero).

For bulk reprints of this article, please call (201) 748-8789.

Latin America's Philanthropic Traditions

Lilya Wagner

Philanthropy and Social Change in Latin America, edited by
Cynthia Sanborn and Felipe Portocarrero. Cambridge, Mass.:
Harvard University Press, 2006. 480 pp., $24.95 paper.

*New Patterns for Mexico: Observations on Remittances, Philan-
thropic Giving, and Equitable Development,* edited by Barbara
J. Merz. Cambridge, Mass.: Harvard University Press, 2006.
312 pp., $19.95 paper.

O NLY A DECADE AGO, when attention on Hispanic or Latino philanthropy and fundraising in the United States was growing,
few books on the topic were available. Just as scarce were
publications that featured Latin American countries and their philanthropic traditions and practices. In the ensuing decade, a number
of academic researchers and their institutions have placed increasing
emphasis on remedying this scarcity of literature that examines philanthropy in Mexico, Central America, and South America. The two
books reviewed here, *Philanthropy and Social Change in Latin America*
and *New Patterns for Mexico: Observations on Remittances, Philanthropic
Giving, and Equitable Development,* are thoughtful presentations of historical perspectives as well as current practices, supported by
research, and therefore welcome additions to the now-swelling information pool available on the topic. For many of us who have long
held positive opinions and views on the generosity of Latin peoples,
these volumes verify our beliefs and experiences and showcase how
philanthropy has flourished and functioned while not always recognized in Western terms.

Philanthropy and Social Change in Latin America, edited by
Cynthia Sanborn and Felipe Portocarrero, is valuable as a reference
replete with examples from which readers can select those chapters
or portions of most relevance or interest, although reading the book
from cover to cover is most beneficial due to the thoughtful presen-
tation of facts, examples, and analyses. It is also a thorough treatment
by the participating authors of Latin American philanthropy in historical terms, current philanthropic practice, the contribution of corporations and their emphasis on social responsibility, the function

NONPROFIT MANAGEMENT & LEADERSHIP, vol. 17, no. 2, Winter 2006 © 2006 Wiley Periodicals, Inc.
Published online in Wiley InterScience (www.interscience.wiley.com). DOI: 10.1002/nml.146

and growth of foundations, and comparative thoughts on Latin America and international practice.

Latin America is often characterized as behind the times in progressive social change and burdened by immense social deficits. The question presented in this book is: If governments with their massive resources of money and manpower have not succeeded, what can private individuals, groups, and organizations possibly accomplish? The authors and editors seek to determine whether and how philanthropy and volunteerism might contribute to the resolution of social issues, and therefore do more than just examine philanthropic practice. They equate both the historical examination as well as current activity and its effect on individual societies and Latin America as a whole. While acknowledging social obstacles, they address the possibility of how these can be overcome in both the quantitative and qualitative roles philanthropy plays.

These volumes . . . showcase how philanthropy [in Latin America] has flourished and functioned while not always recognized in Western terms.

From a purely quantitative sense, the authors acknowledge that philanthropy and volunteering, particularly when compared to U.S. effectiveness and practice, can never provide sufficient material and human resources to change Latin American societies, even though historically Latin American philanthropy and volunteering have often been underestimated. However, in a qualitative sense, philanthropy can play a significant role as a catalyst, energizer, and model builder. The chapters in this book suggest five key philanthropic activities that can accelerate social progress in Latin America:

- Philanthropy can play a key role in communicating, networking, and benchmarking.
- Philanthropy can engage in experimentation and modeling.
- Private philanthropies can publicize and promote proliferation of models.
- Philanthropic organizations can leverage their own resources and experience and increase the engagement of others.
- Philanthropy can promote the development of civil societies and formation of social capital.

The chapters are pioneering in a sense since they explore somewhat unknown terrain and thus collectively inform and provoke. This book grew out of more than three years of research and public debate conducted under the auspices of the Program on Philanthropy, Civil Society, and Social Change in the Americas at Harvard University, jointly sponsored by the David Rockefeller Center for Latin American Studies and the Hauser Center for Nonprofit Organizations. One objective was to increase the understanding of Latin America's philanthropic and voluntary traditions, identify which factors shape or hinder the growth of philanthropy, and examine what happens today by presenting both research and anecdotal evidence.

To accomplish this ambitious goal, chapters in four main categories are included. First is past and present Latin American philanthropy. Often thought to be absent from the Latin American scene, philanthropy in various forms (not necessarily as defined by North American standards) has existed for centuries. Acknowledging this is vital for any contemporary discussion. From this basis, the chapters address the role corporations play, particularly as corporate social responsibility has taken on the form of a movement in Latin America and functions within a broader political and economic context than visible even a decade ago. Also in the past decade there has been a trend toward creation of private foundations. Included in this section is a consideration of the inequities of wealth among Latin American populations and how various factors come into play when motivating people to donate time and resources. The formal regulatory frameworks explored in these chapters greatly increase a comparative understanding of what is possible and what is not in the development of individual giving. Finally, an understanding of differences in organized philanthropy in the United States and Latin America provides perspectives as well as lessons for practitioners on both continents and makes it possible to learn from one another.

The impressive array of authors who have based their chapters on solid research makes this a significant contribution to literature on Latin American philanthropy. While definitely an academic tome, it provides a solid foundation for any practitioner, were he or she to read it in entirety or to peruse those particular sections that are immediately relevant, such as corporate philanthropic development or examples from a specific country.

New Patterns for Mexico, which complements *Philanthropy and Social Changes in Latin America,* addresses how the growing migration from Mexico to the United States has changed and reshaped patterns of giving. Although traditions of philanthropy in Mexico have roots dating back to pre-Hispanic times, the concept and practice of remittances—cross-border flow of giving into Mexico—has grown significantly. Migrant philanthropy, practiced by groups known as hometown associations (HTAs), focuses on raising money for communities of origin in Mexico. Under the rubric of remittances are both family aid and community development. While recognized by all parties, including the Mexican government, as being highly significant in mitigating social causes, migrant giving also generates questions: What is the role of the state? What are the consequences for local governance? What is the sustainability factor of this type of giving? Thus, this book addresses two major questions: How can equitable development be defined, and how does that definition apply to Mexico? In an attempt to lay the groundwork, a section in the introduction enlightens the reader on how equitable development is defined, how it differs from equalities, and how some of Mexico's key equity challenges can be understood. Movement across borders and giving back to a community are ancient traditions, but given the scale of today's activity, in human and economic terms, current cross-border giving from the United States to Mexico is particularly relevant for development.

The impressive array of authors who have based their chapters on solid research makes this a significant contribution to literature on Latin American philanthropy.

The chapters that follow the book's introduction represent various perspectives while sharing defined principles. To establish a basis, an analysis of data collected in 2004 is presented that helps us understand the impact of remittances at the microlevel. Themes that follow include how reform of Mexico's banking sector influences equitable development, particularly as access to Mexico's financial system becomes available for rural communities, and how both financial institutions and foundations in the United States and Mexico could aid in the availability of financial services for migrants and their communities of origin.

Subsequent chapters include a consideration of how current inequities have been propagated because of minority control of Mexico's political power and resources and how political decentralization and remittances can contribute to more democratic local governance. Another chapter uses selected HTA projects in Jerez, Zacatecas, as a framework for HTA development projects. Finally, the evolution of philanthropic activity in Mexico as spurred by the role of leading American foundations discusses how such foundations can play a pivotal role in advancing equity, even though the full potential of this phenomenon is not yet realized. In conclusion, the question of likely consequences for individuals, families, and communities in Mexico should remittances lessen or even disappear is addressed.

This book is unique in that chapters are in both English and Spanish, and there is acknowledgment that the chapters are part of a continuing discussion. The chapters attempt to aid in the understanding of and implications for policy and practice for cross-border philanthropy. As indicated in the Preface, each chapter can be a stand-alone piece for those interested in a specific research agenda, while the book is also intended to inspire debate and dialogue in both Mexico and the United States on how to increase the quantity and effectiveness of resources dedicated to equitable development in Mexico.

Through its Global Philanthropy Program, Harvard's Global Equity Initiative aims to advance knowledge about global philanthropy. This book, one of a series on diaspora giving, greatly enhances current knowledge of Latin American philanthropy and increases understanding of the rather novel and emerging pattern of cross-border flow and its impact on equitable development in Mexico.

Both books are of significant importance and relevance in understanding, participating in, and disseminating information about Latin American philanthropy, and at the same time serve the purpose of dispelling myths while providing research and practice-based knowledge.

> *Both books . . . serve the purpose of dispelling myths while providing research and practice-based knowledge.*

LILYA WAGNER is vice president for philanthropy at Counterpart International, Washington, D.C.

For bulk reprints of this article, please call (201) 748-8789.

A Primer on Fiscal Sponsorship

Michael L. Wyland

Fiscal Sponsorship: Six Ways to Do It Right, 2nd ed., by Gregory
L. Colvin. San Francisco: Study Center Press, 2006. 120 pp.,
$29.95 cloth, $19.95 paper.

MANY INDIVIDUALS and groups wish to pursue a nonprofit mission but lack the organizational infrastructure to establish or maintain a nonprofit corporation. *Fiscal Sponsorship* is a good primer for established nonprofit organizations that might provide this support.

Gregory Colvin originally wrote this book in 1993 to present ethical and legal alternatives to the concept of fiscal agency. Some nonprofits that were asked to be fiscal agents were being used as conduits or pass-through agencies for individuals or groups to receive tax-deductible contributions to fund activities of questionable public benefit. As a result, the terms *fiscal agency* and *fiscal agent,* as applied to nonprofits, have become suspect. *Fiscal sponsorship* is the preferred term for proper arrangements between nonprofits and those seeking the benefits of nonprofit incorporation for public benefit purposes.

The book outlines three scenarios: two artists seeking charitable support for their artistic production and teaching activities; a church with an AIDS hospice program that has outgrown the church's capacity to manage it effectively; and a U.S. environmental group with significant lobbying activities seeking to purchase Brazilian rain forest to protect it from development. Each scenario is then applied to six fiscal sponsorship models in ascending order of independence and autonomy. A handy two-page reference chart compares and contrasts the six models, supplementing the book's narrative. A seventh model, derived from a 1990 U.S. Supreme Court decision specific to Mormon (LDS Church) parents providing tax-deductible support for their children's mission activities, is explored but noted to be as yet untested.

My own ethical antennas were alerted when the AIDS hospice scenario included a desire by friends and relatives to make tax-deductible gifts to support a specific patient's medication needs. I would have been more comfortable had Colvin handled this potentially dangerous issue more regularly and consistently throughout the book's application of each sponsorship model to the scenarios. He alludes to the Internal Revenue Service's requirement for a

tax-deductible gift to benefit an indefinite, open-ended "charitable class" when discussing a preapproved grantor-grantee relationship, but does not address the issue equally well when discussing the other five models.

A Web site, www.fiscalsponsorship.com, has been set up in conjunction with the second edition of the book. Unfortunately, the Web site seeks only to sell the book and provides links to two other Web sites with sponsorship-related information—far from the promise of posting new developments in fiscal sponsorship.

> *The book outlines three scenarios. . . . Each scenario is then applied to six fiscal sponsorship models.*

This book is not for the casual reader. Most people and groups in need of fiscal sponsorship will likely not know how to articulate that need and will be less sophisticated in evaluating the legal and operational considerations. However, representatives of organizations seeking brief, solid advice on options for supporting nonprofit activities of smaller groups and individuals will find it very helpful.

MICHAEL L. WYLAND *is a partner at Sumption & Wyland, a business consulting firm in Sioux Falls, South Dakota.*

For bulk reprints of this article, please call (201) 748-8789.

BULLETIN BOARD

February 2007

21 National Council for Voluntary Organisations Annual Conference, The Brewery, London, e-mail: gillen.knight@ncvo-vol.org.uk, http://www.ncvo-vol.org.uk

26–28 Child Welfare League of America National Conference, "Raising Our Voices for Children," Marriott Wardman Park, Washington, D.C., http://www.cwla.org/conferences

March 2007

1–2 Nonprofit Legal & Tax Conference, J. W. Marriott Hotel, Washington, D.C., http://www.taxexemptresources.com

12–13 European Institute for Advanced Studies in Management, "Challenges of Managing the Third Sector," Venice International University, Venice, Italy, e-mail: audrey@eiasm.be, http://www.eiasm.org

15–17 Hands On Network Leadership Conference, "Seeds of Change: Cultivating Active Citizens Through Service," Sheraton New Orleans, http://www.handsonnetwork.org

23–27 American Society for Public Administration National Conference, "Monumental Possibilities: Capitalizing on Cooperation," Washington, D.C., http://www.aspanet.org

25–28 Association of Fundraising Professionals, International Conference on Fundraising, Dallas, Texas, tel.: 703–684–0410, http://www.afpnet.org

April 2007

4–6 Nonprofit Technology Conference, "Reinventing Politics: Creating Social Change from the Ground Up," Omni Shoreham Hotel, Washington, D.C., http://nten.org/ntc

17–19 Social Enterprise Alliance Conference, Hyatt Regency, Long Beach, California, http://www.se-alliance.org/events_gathering8.cfm

25–28 Urban Affairs Association Annual Conference, Westin Seattle, e-mail: uaa@udel.edu, http://www.udel.edu/uaa

July 2007

18–20 Alliance for Nonprofit Management Conference, Atlanta, Georgia, http://www.allianceonline.org

August 2007

11–14 American Sociological Association Annual Meeting, "Is Another World Possible? Sociological Perspectives on Contemporary Politics," Hilton New York and Sheraton New York, http://www.asanet.org

October 2007

24–26 Risk Management and Finance Summit for Nonprofits, Winston-Salem, North Carolina, http://nonprofitrisk.org

27–30 Council on Social Work Education Conference, "Preparing the Next Generation of Educators," Hilton San Francisco, e-mail: apm@cswe.org, http://www.cswe.org

November 2007

15–17 Association for Research on Nonprofit Organizations and Voluntary Action (ARNOVA) Annual Conference, Omni Hotel, Atlanta, tel.: 317–684–2120, fax: 317–684–2128, http://www.arnova.org

Nonprofit Management and Leadership welcomes queries or finished papers from both scholars and practitioners. Submitted papers should be 4,000 to 5,000 words in length and based on original research or theory of organizations and management. Papers should be written in a jargon-free, nontechnical style accessible to managers, trustees, and other leaders of nonprofit and voluntary organizations as well as academic researchers and teachers from a variety of disciplines. The focus should be on some aspect of nonprofit organization management or leadership, especially governance, management of human resources, resource development and financial management, strategy and management of change, and organizational effectiveness. Readers' reactions to articles and features in *NML* are also welcomed. Please send your observations in the form of a one-page letter for possible publication in the Commentary section. Authors are also encouraged to submit short case studies (2,500 words or fewer) for the Feature section.

Electronic submissions in MS Word format are preferred; e-mail manuscripts and comments as file attachments to

Kathleen Mills, Managing Editor, at NMLjournal@case.edu

Otherwise, send one copy of the manuscript (with accompanying electronic copy on disk, if possible) via the post to

Roger A. Lohmann, Editor
Nonprofit Management and Leadership
Mandel Center for Nonprofit Organizations
Case Western Reserve University
10900 Euclid Avenue
Cleveland, OH 44106-7167

Manuscript Preparation

Type all copy double-spaced—including references and extracts—leaving margins at least one inch wide. The title page should include the title of the article, the names and primary affiliations of the author(s), and a brief abstract. To facilitate the blind review process, make sure information about authors appears only on the title page. Spell out *e.g., i.e., et al., . . .* to their English equivalents and avoid complex mathematical symbols when possible.

Citations and References. Do not use footnotes. For literature citations in text, supply author surname and date of publication and include the original page number for each direct quotation and statistic. For example: Knight (1973) or Knight and Jones (1975, p. 74). Provide a *double-spaced* alphabetized list of only those references cited in the text, using the following style:

Journal Article

Aussieker, B., and Garbarino, J. W. "Measuring Faculty Unionism: Quantity and Quality." *Industrial Relations,* 1973, *12*(1), 117–124.

Book

Abbot, F. C. *Government Policy and Higher Education.* Ithaca, N.Y.: Cornell University Press, 1958.

Chapter in a Book

Riesman, D., and Jencks, C. "The Viability of the American College." In N. Sanford (ed.), *The American College: A Psychological and Social Interpretation of Higher Learning.* New York: Wiley, 1962.

Refer to current issues of *NML* for additional guidance.

Figures and Tables. Figures are best submitted in TIFF or EPS (with preview) formats. If these formats are not possible, use JPEG. Figures can also be submitted in MS Word if necessary. Tables should be typed double-spaced on separate pages, and table notes should be keyed to the body of the table with letters rather than numbers or asterisks. All figures and tables should have short descriptive titles.

For more information, please request a copy of *NML's Guidelines for Authors.*

Publication Process

After a manuscript is accepted for publication, authors are asked to sign a letter of agreement granting the publisher the right to copyedit, publish, and copyright the material. The editor is responsible for proofreading each issue and will only contact authors if clarification is needed; copyedited manuscripts will not be returned to authors. Authors must ensure the accuracy of all statements—particularly data, quotations, and references—before submitting manuscripts.

We gratefully acknowledge the generous support and encouragement of the Mandel Foundation. Established by Jack, Joseph, and Morton Mandel of Cleveland, Ohio, the Mandel Foundation's primary mission is to help provide outstanding leadership for the nonprofit sector.

ORDERING INFORMATION

SUBSCRIPTION rates: For institutions, agencies, and libraries: $212 per year in the United States, $252 per year in Canada and Mexico, and $286 per year in the rest of the world for the print version; $212 worldwide for the electronic version; and $234 in the United States, $274 in Canada and Mexico, and $308 in the rest of the world for both the print and the electronic versions. For individuals: $80 per year in the United States, Canada, and Mexico and $104 per year in the rest of the world. Prices subject to change. To ensure correct and prompt delivery, all orders must give either the name of an individual or an official purchase order number.

To place an order:

By mail, write to Customer Service, Jossey-Bass, 989 Market Street, San Francisco, CA 94103-1741.

By phone, call toll-free (888) 378-2537 or call (415) 433-1740.

By fax, dial toll-free (888) 481-2665.

Visit our Web site at www.josseybass.com

United States Postal Service

Statement of Ownership, Management, and Circulation

1. Publication Title	2. Publication Number	3. Filing Date
Nonprofit Management & Leadership	1 0 4 8 _ 6 6 8 2	10/1/06

4. Issue Frequency	5. Number of Issues Published Annually	6. Annual Subscription Price
Quarterly	4	$212.00

7. Complete Mailing Address of Known Office of Publication *(Not printer) (Street, city, county, state, and ZIP+4)*	Contact Person Joe Schuman
Wiley Subscription Services, Inc. at Jossey-Bass, 989 Market Street, San Francisco, CA 94103	Telephone (415) 782-3232

8. Complete Mailing Address of Headquarters or General Business Office of Publisher *(Not printer)*

Wiley Subscription Services, Inc. 111 River Street, Hoboken, NJ 07030

9. Full Names and Complete Mailing Addresses of Publisher, Editor, and Managing Editor *(Do not leave blank)*

Publisher *(Name and complete mailing address)*

Wiley Subscriptions Services, Inc., A Wiley Company at San Francisco, 989 Market Street, San Francisco, CA 94103-1741

Editor *(Name and complete mailing address)*

Roger A. Lohmann, Mandel Center for Nonprofit Org., Case Western Univ., 10900 Euclid Avenue, Cleveland, OH 44106

Managing Editor *(Name and complete mailing address)*

None

10. Owner *(Do not leave blank. If the publication is owned by a corporation, give the name and address of the corporation immediately followed by the names and addresses of all stockholders owning or holding 1 percent or more of the total amount of stock. If not owned by a corporation, give the names and addresses of the individual owners. If owned by a partnership or other unincorporated firm, give its name and address as well as those of each individual owner. If the publication is published by a nonprofit organization, give its name and address.)*

Full Name	Complete Mailing Address
Wiley Subscription Services, Inc.	111 River Street, Hoboken, NJ 07030
(see attached list)	

11. Known Bondholders, Mortgagees, and Other Security Holders Owning or Holding 1 Percent or More of Total Amount of Bonds, Mortgages, or Other Securities. If none, check box ➤ ☑ None

Full Name	Complete Mailing Address
None	None

12. Tax Status *(For completion by nonprofit organizations authorized to mail at nonprofit rates) (Check one)*
The purpose, function, and nonprofit status of this organization and the exempt status for federal income tax purposes:
☐ Has Not Changed During Preceding 12 Months
☐ Has Changed During Preceding 12 Months *(Publisher must submit explanation of change with this statement)*

13. Publication Title Nonprofit Management & Leadership	14. Issue Date for Circulation Data Below Summer 2006

15.		Extent and Nature of Circulation	Average No. Copies Each Issue During Preceding 12 Months	No. Copies of Single Issue Published Nearest to Filing Date
a.		Total Number of Copies *(Net press run)*	1546	913
b. Paid and/or Requested Circulation	(1)	Paid/Requested Outside-County Mail Subscriptions Stated on Form 3541. *(Include advertiser's proof and exchange copies)*	575	574
	(2)	Paid In-County Subscriptions Stated on Form 3541 *(Include advertiser's proof and exchange copies)*	0	0
	(3)	Sales Through Dealers and Carriers, Street Vendors, Counter Sales, and Other Non-USPS Paid Distribution	0	0
	(4)	Other Classes Mailed Through the USPS	0	0
c.		Total Paid and/or Requested Circulation *[Sum of 15b. (1), (2),(3),and (4)]* ➤	575	574
d. Free Distribution by Mail (Samples, compliment ary, and other free)	(1)	Outside-County as Stated on Form 3541	0	0
	(2)	In-County as Stated on Form 3541	0	0
	(3)	Other Classes Mailed Through the USPS	0	0
e.		Free Distribution Outside the Mail *(Carriers or other means)*	55	58
f.		Total Free Distribution *(Sum of 15d. and 15e.)* ➤	55	58
g.		Total Distribution *(Sum of 15c. and 15f)* ➤	630	632
h.		Copies not Distributed	660	281
i.		Total *(Sum of 15g. and h.)* ➤	1290	913
j.		Percent Paid and/or Requested Circulation *(15c. divided by 15g. times 100)*	91%	91%

16. Publication of Statement of Ownership
☑ Publication required. Will be printed in the Winter 2006 issue of this publication.   ☐ Publication not required.

17. Signature and Title of Editor, Publisher, Business Manager, or Owner	Date
Susan E. Lewis, VP & Publisher - Periodicals *(signature)*	10/01/06

I certify that all information furnished on this form is true and complete. I understand that anyone who furnishes false or misleading information on this form or who omits material or information requested on the form may be subject to criminal sanctions (including fines and imprisonment) and/or civil sanctions (including civil penalties).

Notes

Notes